REACHIN
the OVERSOUL

REACHING for
the OVERSOUL

A True Story of a Physician and his Patient
Hypnotic Regression—Seeking the Eternal Friend
Encounter with Yan Su Lu—The Healing Factor

Introduction by Elisabeth Kübler-Ross, M. D.

Eugene G. Jussek, M.D.

NICOLAS~HAYS, INC.
York Beach, Maine

First published in 1994 by
Nicolas-Hays, Inc.
P. O. Box 612
York Beach, ME 03910-0612

Distributed to the trade by
Samuel Weiser, Inc.
P. O. Box 612
York Beach, ME 03910-0612

Library of Congress Cataloging-in-Publication Data
Jussek, Eugene G.
        Reaching for the oversoul / by Eugene G. Jussek.
            p.   cm.
        Includes bibliographical references and index.
        1. Hypnotism--Case studies.   2. Reincarnation--Case studies.
    3. Guides (Spiritualism)   I. Title.
    BF1156.R45J87   1994   94-17740
    133.9'01'3--dc20   CIP

ISBN 0-89254-027-3
CCP

Cover art is a painting titled "Remember," by Nicholas Roerich. Copyright © 1994. Used by kind permission of the Nicholas Roerich Museum, New York.

Typeset in 11 point Palatino

Printed in the United States of America

99 98 97 96 95 94
10 9 8 7 6 5 4 3 2 1

The paper used in this publication meets the minimum requirements of the American National Standard for Permanence of Paper for Printed Library Materials Z39.48-1984.

My thanks to Charles Roberts for sharing his experience with us, and for giving his permission to publish this book. I thank Dorothy and Jennifer for their loving support.

My thanks go also to Maya and Nicole, as well as to my special friends for their gracious help.

TABLE OF CONTENTS

A Note to the Reader

This book concerns itself with the possible existence of past lives and a guardian consciousness which oversees the individual's inner development from life to life.

Ever since I was a young child and witnessed my beloved grandfather's death and burial . . . ever since, as a young draftee, I had to watch in shock and disbelief the senseless sacrifice of human life in World War II . . . ever since I observed the fragility of this body in the decades of my medical practice . . . certain questions burned in my mind:

- What is the reason for the body, this vessel for the infinitely precious essence, when it is so easily destroyed?

- Is death the end of life?

- What is life everlasting?

- Where is its beginning?

- What part do we play in the masterplan of life?

The search for understanding took me to the remote corners of the Earth and led me to many teachers. But there were few souls evolved enough to show me the answers.

Over the years many patients have come to me in pain and confusion. In my efforts to help, I came to see the importance of right attitude, of striving to hear the voice of the wiser self within. I increased the use of hypnosis in my practice because I knew that many potential troubles are caused by wrong attitude and are present long before they show up in the physical body. Once detected, they can often be corrected and the patient enabled to help him- or herself.

During this work I came upon a young man who was deeply troubled by a behavior problem for which he had no explanation. I decided to hypnotically regress him into past life experiences. I was intrigued by the wealth of detail that came out during the hypnosis. Although it is not my intention to prove or disprove the possibility of reincarnation in this book, two of the past life experiences of my patient were close enough in time to enable me to research the data that was disclosed in the sessions. I went to England to try to verify information given under hypnosis about a lifetime there in the 19th century. In historical archives, as well as the local parish, we located birth and death records, names, dates, relationships, professions; we found buildings and documentation of their former uses, names of schools no longer in existence, addresses of residences long since torn down. In an amazing number of instances, the details checked out with the hypnotic data.

My family and I also traveled to Ireland, where the patient had experienced an 18th century life as a rebel against the British, but we were told that all records for this period had been lost. We managed, however, to verify much of the hypnotic data about the living conditions, starvation, village organization, and desperate farmers who made themselves into cadres of soldiers.

During regressions we observed a peculiar thing: the patient's apparent recognition of a separate entity who seemed to have been present at his death, whom my patient called his friend and teacher. The views this "entity" offered on subjects such as reincarnation, death, suicide, birth, reasons for being, love, success, all came without the slightest hesitation. Most provocative was his insistence that everyone has a guardian or teacher.

I have known Doctor Eugene Jussek for a good many years. As a highly respected physician of the State of California, he has used much of his own time and money to research new approaches and methods in the field of internal medicine, adding several of his own.

As a teenager he had been drafted into the German armed forces and served on the Eastern German fronts of World War 2. Subsequently he completed his medical training at the university of Frankfurt/Main. He supplemented his studies in New York City, including post graduate work at the world renowned New York University Bellevue Medical Center. Later he established his practice in Los Angeles, California, where over the past decades he has been widely consulted for his considerable expertise.

Because of his impressive scientific background, I was struck at once by his wide-ranging interest in the metaphysical, a field in which I have done considerable investigating over the years. Unlike many who come from similar educational disciplines, he had an open, venturing mind, knowing from his experience as a medical doctor that there was more to life than a surgeon's scalpel could probe.

Like myself, he was a student of life, in all its possible forms. Believing in God and everything He had created, he did not limit God's universe to the limitations of the conscious mind.

As a scientist, he recognized that where there was a result—or consequence—there must also be a cause. He searched for that cause, first in the interest of the patient who was suffering from disorders for which there seemed to be no apparent cause, and then again in its more general application to the mysteries of life. Knowing from his practice that many illnesses were induced by the mind, he ventured into its deeper layers—the memory banks of the subconscious—in his quest for the solution to a patient's troubled body and mind.

He would regress patients, when indicated, through the art of hypnosis, into the hazy past, into almost forgotten childhoods, and patients would speak, sometimes haltingly, of traumatic incidents upon which their conscious minds had put a lid over the passage of time. But an unusual—even mindboggling—dimension was to be added to this therapy, for, as Dr. Jussek regressed his patients, they frequently would go back beyond childhood into their mother's womb, where they had an early consciousness they shared with their mother. And then, a step further, into past life experience in which they assumed different external identities, lived in different people. And yet, it was all connected to the present, and the life they led in this experience, with all its pains and pleasures. It was causative as well. For just as Dr. Jussek was able to find some traumatic origin for a patient's illness in an earlier experience in this life, he was able to trace disorders and diseases to equally traumatic episodes in the memory bank of a past life experience. It was an exciting discovery which opened the door to his far-reaching exploration of the whole concept of rebirth and one continuous life. Are we here merely to live out one existence, so often in purposeless drudgery? Or are we granted the God-given opportunity to learn from the past, and to develop capacities and traits at the same time to carry with us karmically, as they say in the East, into a purposeful existence, shaped by our every thought and action?

In his book, Dr. Jussek examines the possibility of reincarnation and the access to a higher wisdom available to us all. He brings the zest of a scientist and the art of a dramatist as he shares with us the richness of his own experience. This is a fascinating study, from which many may profit by opening their minds and souls. Above all, this book is a metaphysical journey which will make many people think, realizing that there is no limitation to life but life itself.

PREFACE

Q: After you died, what happened to your soul?

A: I was met by my wonderful friend. I do not know him by his name. He is ageless. Immediately after death we would speak of my experiences of that lifetime and the lessons that were learned.

Q: Did you ask him about God?

A: It is always the same—that God is infinite.

My deeply hypnotized patient was talking in an even, matter-of-fact voice, telling me how he had died after a life as a Mexican girl hundreds of years ago. Over a period of weeks I had regressed my intense subject, Charles Roberts, into a number of vivid and varied past lives that had the feel of reality, as I searched for the roots of his present problems.

As our efforts progressed I experienced with Charles a gamut of strong emotions—grief, happiness, torture, regret—and in every remembered life he had unhesitatingly described his own death, almost with a sense of relief. After recounting some of the painful memories, his voice would change and he would speak of his reassuring meetings beyond death with this special person he called his friend and teacher.

Now, I'm not easily surprised by anything on this earth, or even beyond it. For more than twenty years I have been using medical hypnosis in my practice, and I have encountered many unusual personalities outside the scope of physical sight or simple explanations. But Charles' insistence under trance that there was a personal teacher waiting to help him each time he died was something new to my experience as a physician, and completely fascinating.

The idea itself was not new to me. I had long pondered the puzzles of consciousness, the existence of soul, the uniqueness of human individuality, the possibility of life after death, the kindly figure of light reported by those who have survived clinical death, and especially the interim periods between lives in connection with the theory of reincarnation.

Charles' continued references to his discarnate teacher were intriguing enough to provoke the sleuth in me, and my curiosity led me into a strange situation indeed: a series of philosophic conversations with the "friend and teacher" himself, a dignified Chinese personality who spoke through Charles and called himself Yan Su Lu.

As a human being I am keenly interested and open regarding the world's religious philosophies, while as a medical doctor I feel obligated to be cautious about material presented to me through hypnosis. For almost two years these conversations continued until I had amassed several notebooks full of transcripts of Yan Su Lu's teachings.

The landscapes of the inner mind are not easily charted, and the sources of knowledge are not to be assigned to convenient categories. I agree wholeheartedly with Robert Ornstein, the innovative transpersonal researcher, who feels that we live in a time when "a new and extended conception of man is beginning to emerge, one which includes many capacities beyond the normal limits."[1]

And so, questions must always be asked and asked again. Amazing phenomena may have prosaic explanations, paranormal experiences must be observed with a cool eye; yet spiritual intuition must not be shut out by the purely scientific approach.

With that caveat I feel I can present the case of Charles Roberts, my conversations with Yan Su Lu, and the events that led up to them. I trust that the reader will take what is valuable to his or her spiritual growth and let the rest go, with the realization that we, all of us, are yet imperfect travelers on a very long and very challenging path of evolution.

---

[1] Robert Ornstein: *The Psychology of Consciousness*, 2nd ed., New York: Harcourt Brace, 1977.

INTRODUCTION

by Elisabeth Kübler-Ross

This is a remarkable and special book, written by an extremely well-trained scientist and physician with an analytical, critical mind and years of clinical experience.

When Dr. Jussek used hypnotherapy and hypnotic regression with his patients, he unexpectedly discovered more and more remarkable things—matters that would be frowned upon in our medical institutions. Instead of dismissing these things, he continued his work and was open and bold enough to share his findings with the world.

Jussek is a skeptical researcher who carefully checks his data and who didn't hesitate to travel far to confirm (or refute) his information. What he shares in this book is something of which many people are only marginally aware, although all of us are on the same path of spiritual evolution. Many of his statements will ring true to the evolved reader, while others will dismiss them with some judgmental label.

I can only confirm that the greatest part of the book, especially the chapter "Dying, Suicide, and Guardian Angels," has been verified by my own research of death and life after death. I have also experienced many of these things myself in my search for answers during the past two decades.

Our teachers are always there to guide us—from the moment of birth and on through life and the transition we call death. They are not able, however, to interfere with our free choice, God's greatest gift. This makes us totally responsible for all of our choices—our deeds, our words, our thoughts. "As you sow, so shall you reap," is an absolute truth all of us need to accept.

This book also describes beautifully the general purpose of life, again confirmed by my research. That purpose is to find a true balance of the mental, physical, and spiritual aspects of human existence on our planet Earth (I call it "to live in harmony with the physical, emotional, intellectual, and spiritual quadrants"), thus to become Christlike in our spiritual evolution. With love as the basis of life, manifested as tolerance, understanding, and an ever-increasing sensitivity, a growing person can achieve an openness that will help him not only to understand this book, but to acknowledge the guidance of our heavenly teachers, whether we see them as coming from within or without.

Thank you for the privilege of reviewing and introducing this remarkable book.

In each of us there is another whom we do not know. He speaks to us in dreams and tells us how differently he sees us from the way we see ourselves. When, therefore, we find ourselves in a difficult situation to which there is no solution, he can sometimes kindle a light that radically alters our attitude—the very attitude that led us into the difficult situation.

Together the patient and I address ourselves to the 2,000,000-year-old man that is in all of us. In the last analysis, most of our difficulties come from losing contact with our instincts, with the age-old unforgotten wisdom stored up in us. And where do we make contact with this old man in us? In our dreams.

C.G. Jung
Psychological Reflections, p. 76

REACHING for the OVERSOUL

CHAPTER 1

My Own Journey

"At some level of the universe we are all interconnected . . . to each other and to all other things."

Dr. William A. Tiller, Physicist

"INTO WHATSOEVER HOUSE I SHALL ENTER . . ."

—from the Hippocratic Oath

My mother's father, George, was dying. He had always been a healthy man, but now nuns in black robes prayed at his bedside. At times he screamed because the pain in his heart was unbearable. I was 10 years old and it was the first time death had come close to me.

As I watched, his face suddenly lost all expression, as though it had just turned to stone. It was a beautiful face still, but the person who had been my grandfather was no longer there. This must be it, I thought. Death. I felt frightened, unable to truly understand what had just happened.

Later, they dressed my grandfather in a clean nightgown and changed the bed sheets. They closed his eyes and folded his hands. The room was quiet in a way that I had never experienced before. Then men came, all dressed in black, and took my grandfather away.

It was a gray day when I stood with my family in the graveyard. I couldn't help staring into the deep hole before us while the priest spoke. The casket was lowered by ropes into the soil dark with moisture from the morning rain, and my grandfather was buried. I would never again see the person I had known so well. The thought ran through my body like an electric shock, and I began to cry.

Later, I asked my mother what all this meant, and what had really happened to grandfather.

"I am sure he is in heaven now," she said. "He was a good man. You see, you, too, were taught to pray and when your time comes, you will also go to heaven."

"But what will happen to people who are not good?" I demanded. "Do they go to hell and stay there forever? The priest seems to think so."

My mother looked thoughtful and did not answer me. I felt then that I would not rest until I could find an answer to this question.

I cannot ignore the many strange coincidences that have happened to me. Events have had a way of turning suddenly in new directions to change the course of my life, or I have been drawn to special bits of skill and knowledge that years later would prove to be vital to my well-being, even to my very existence.

Even though my childhood environment was conservative, it was one that fostered intellectual exploration. I remember how my mind was constantly reaching out for more understanding. Very early in life I became a voracious reader. During my first years at the Johann Wolfgang Goethe Gymnasium in Frankfurt, my home town, I was spellbound by accounts of the extraordinary powers of the lamas and yogis of Tibet and India, about whom I read. The books of Madame Alexandra David-Neel fascinated me. She wrote of her years in Tibet and the disciplines she learned from the holy men there.

I read detailed descriptions of Tibetan monks who were able to generate great heat inside their bodies so that, while wrapped in wet clothes and lying upon a frozen lake, they used this inner heat to completely dry out the cloth. The exercise, called Tumo, demonstrated the mind's ability to control the autonomic nervous system and has recently been further substantiated by Herbert Benson, M.D., who, in his book, *Beyond the Relaxation Response*, describes in detail his studies of Tibetan monks in the Himalayas and their remarkable abilities to control autonomic processes by will.[1]

---

[1] Herbert Benson, M.D., *Beyond the Relaxation Response*, New York: Times Books, 1984.

I decided to practice the discipline on myself. While in a meditative state I visualized a fire burning inside my body. Now, breathing in a certain manner I increased the heat, using my lungs as a bellows to fan the flame. For months I did this by progressive stages until it was time to put myself to a critical test. I was 14 years old and had great faith in my ability to take on any challenge.

In that icy cold winter I swam across the river Main and back, unaffected by the freezing temperature. It worked! After that, whenever I was in the Swiss Alps I would look for a mountain lake, find a spot which was not solidly covered with ice, remove my clothes, and immerse myself to the neck in the water.

My body became more and more proficient at producing heat at will and I tested this by extending the time I was able to remain in the icy water. That this technique would one day save my life, I could not know at the time. Nor did I realize how deeply involved I was to become in the mysterious relationship between the mind and body.[2]

Ours was a traditional German family. My mother was a strong and beautiful woman whom I adored, and the world of my childhood was an orderly one—church, home, school.

My father was a banker, who, because of his political foresight, helped many of his Jewish colleagues to escape Germany,

---

[2] This experiment on my own body taught me at an early age that the nervous system, which we call autonomic, can be made subject to voluntary control through conditioning.

This concept has been known in yoga since ancient times and has been practiced for the purpose of physiological self-regulation. Modern research supports this knowledge of yoga adepts, that many involuntary processes can be altered, like heartrate, body temperature, blood flow, oxygen consumption, digestive action, etc. (see studies of Elmer Green of the Menninger Clinic on Swami Rama).

This knowledge later became a part of my medical practice. Tumo is a form of autogenic training which was developed by Schultz in Berlin (J.H. Schultz & W. Luthe, *Autogenic Training*, New York: Grune & Stratton, 1951). The progressive relaxation technique of Jacobson is similar to the Schultz method (E. Jacobson, *Progressive Relaxation*, Chicago: University of Chicago Press, 1938). The Silva Mind Control technique also belongs in this category.

and because of his inborn Catholicism, never lost courage in the face of the resulting difficulties. One of four children, he helped his widowed mother support the family when he was 12. The herding instinct he developed while looking after each family member stayed with him, and he became an advisor to an ever-growing family of people.

I liked sports, especially judo, boxing, and field athletics, and I recall being with the University of Frankfurt boxing team when we participated in the All German University Championship at Innsbruck. The memory is especially vivid because I had always loved that alpine city and I used to ski there in the winter whenever I had a chance. I had no intuition then, as I competed with the other boxers, that it would be many years before I would see that beautiful place again, and in that future time, it would be as a man whose orderly world no longer existed.

The war engulfed us all as it swept across Europe. For me it meant having to join the army. I never wanted to be a soldier. I believed that war would bring only misery and could not lead to peace. How could peace be won out of killing and destruction? I hated it.

I was sent to Russia, assigned to a reconnaissance troop of the Mounted Artillery Division of the German Army. We laid and installed the telephone cables to connect the front line infantry and artillery positions. I also served as a courier. Often we had to work under heavy fire, silently approaching on horseback, then going on foot to lay and maintain the lines. Like a jackrabbit, I jumped in and out of foxholes, dashed from cover to cover, working to save my comrades who depended on the lines. All the time I tried to avoid death. It was an instinct having nothing to do with intelligence that saw me through— or perhaps it was a guardian angel.

During the first winter in Russia we did not receive the clothing needed to protect us against the cold. Many soldiers suffered frostbite, often requiring the amputation of arms or legs or feet or hands. Some simply froze to death. At night we slept in the snow, or in crumbling huts, in thin sleeping bags. We stood watch in –40 degree temperature. I was saved from great suffering because I could keep my body warm using the discipline of tumo.

As the great mowing down of human lives proceeded, my inner voice became more insistent. Why should I destroy the gentle people I saw in their villages, in their fields? In a state of helpless shock I watched hundreds of people die all around me. They were gone in a matter of seconds, their bodies dotting the snow like discarded garments. Others were not so lucky, screaming out of their minds with pain and terror. They had to wait in filth and hunger, in cold and wet agony for death to take them. They had been boys like myself, some good, some not so good. During the night watch in the Russian fields, I would gaze at the stars and demand an explanation for all that I had seen. I questioned the very existence of a God who could allow a whole generation of young men, hardly more than children, to die in such misery and indignity.

I felt sorry for the Russian farmers whose fields and livelihood had been destroyed, often their families killed. Yet, an old woman hid me in her hut and saved my life. Why? I was supposed to be the enemy. What was the reason for this? The seeds of philosophy were growing within me now. Life was holy, life was to be celebrated. Each being was unique in every way, not one fingerprint like another. This mind and body—how delicate they were. And here on the vast frozen plains they were cut down like blades of grass. I was filled with love for all these souls, so many of whom had to leave their lives suddenly and violently. What happened to them, I wondered, what happened to the lives they started? And what would happen to those who came through this holocaust alive?

By now I was in charge of a first aid assembly station in the Medical Corps, close to the enemy lines.[3] We hadn't enough pain medication or plasma, antiseptics, or lights. We sorted the dead from the living, wrapped what was left of them in bandages, and loaded them on the panje sleds which periodically took them to some huts behind the lines which served as assembly centers—if they made it. I heard the agony, the screams,

---

[3] As a medical student, I was transferred to the Medical Corps.

the sobs and moans. I heard the silence; there was little I could do. I prayed, I talked to them constantly, giving them my strength, my body, my soul, and it helped. I felt and saw that I could transfer strength with my voice. I was able to make pain more bearable by drawing their attention from it.

Our company marched on to Obojan, a small town north of Charkow.[4] Winter was upon us. The Russian armies had surrounded us. Supplies did not reach us anymore. As had been done to Napoleon was now being done to us. We were cut off. Most of our horses had died and we had eaten their meat. Now I was working in a school basement, assisting an army surgeon by candlelight.

It seemed inconceivable to me that I should ever come out of this nightmare, fighting an enemy who was my brother, watching women and children perish. There was no reason, no excuse, and no way out. Yet in my heart I knew that I would be led out of this, and to my amazement, I was called back from the front to resume my medical studies. The rest of my comrades marched on after the Russian pincer was broken, and at Stalingrad they made their final stand. The fact that I was spared was something I pondered long and deeply.

During the time of my medical training, I explored the ideas of Western thinkers and spiritual teachers. I accepted the challenge of the Greek Heraclitus, who spoke to me from the sixth century B.C.: "You could not discover the limits of the soul even if you travelled by every path in order to do so—such is the depth of its meaning."[5] I found the echo of his words in Carl Gustav Jung who wrote: "Nobody can say where man ends. That is the beauty of it. The unconscious of man can reach God knows where. There we are going to make discoveries."[6]

Many of my fellow physicians tell us to be wary of accepting religious views as scientific, yet, whatever action we take as

---

[4] Obojan is a town located between Kurk and Charkow.

[5] John Sallis & Kenneth Maly, *Heraclitean fragments* (University of Alabama Press, 1980), Fragment 45, p. 62. This is a companion volume of the Heidigger/Fink seminar on Heraclitus.

[6] Jolande Jacobi, ed., *C.G. Jung: Psychological Reflections: A New Anthology of his Writings* (Princeton, NJ: Princeton University Press, 1953, 1970), p. 28.

a result of observing and interpreting life can, in my opinion, be called either scientific or philosophical. Scientists cannot avoid being philosophers because even in the most careful experiment, conclusions must be drawn. Theories are developed which in their final essence influence trends of thought concerning our world, what it is, where it is going. Eventually these conclusions will become part of a philosophy. Einstein's statements about time and space could not be tied into such a tiny package as pure science. He was speaking about the nature of the universe; and so is philosophy, and so is religion.

I have been trained as a scientist, but I cannot explain consciousness. Science is proving little fragments of that great unit of energy that we call consciousness. We cannot see it, only its effects. Some think that it manifests from one part of the brain, but does that prove that the function of the consciousness is purely brain function, or something that works through the brain?

In ancient times there was not such compartmentalized views of science and philosophy. 2,500 years ago Heraclitus the philosopher/scientist said: "The universe is generated not according to time, but according to thought."[7] In this century Sir James Jeans, the British scientist, echoed: "The universe begins to look more like a great thought than a machine."[8] In recent years, the work of the Nobel Prize winning Australian-born neurophysiologist, Sir John Eccles, suggests that non-material energy (thought consciousness) triggers the physical brain, this being only the receiver and not the creator of ideas.[9] Eccles is not alone among prominent scientists in this view. The importance of this experiment is that it builds a bridge between the

---

[7] Commentary on a Fragment of Heraclitus' Teachings, in *Doxographi Greaci* (1879) edited by H. Diels, pp. 273-444.

[8] James Jeans, *The Mysterious Universe* (New York: E.P. Dutton, 1932) quoted in Michael Talbot, *Mysticism and the New Physics* (New York: Bantam, 1981), p. 16.

[9] John Carew Eccles and Daniel N. Robinson, *The Wonder of Being Human: Our Brain, Our Mind*, (New York: The Free Press, Macmillan Co., 1984), p. 162.

scientific and the philosophical views.[10] Though divided by an expanse of time, each of these men dared to look at life with the physical eye—and also with the power of intuition—to see a deeper reality hidden behind the surface of our world.

If we cannot use all of the faculties of our minds, the scientific disciplines as well as a profound search for meaning, then we will not understand the nature of life, or death, or consciousness.

I began my clinical medical training as a resident of the Johann Wolfgang Goethe University, Frankfurt on the Main. I chose the pathology department because I felt it would be important for me to see and feel the pathological changes of the diseased organs and to study them under a microscope. To see the progress of an illness in this way makes a permanent impression on one's brain. This training also brought me in touch with the cellular-pathological viewpoints in medicine expounded by Virchow and his contemporaries.

From pathology, I went into surgery. I wanted to be able to take care of minor and intermediate surgical procedures. I feel that every physician should know how to perform an appendectomy, if needed.

During the following years, I specialized in Internal Medicine, my chosen field, at the Medical Clinic of Frankfurt University. In those years, I was fortunate enough to enjoy an excellent relationship with one of my teachers, the late Professor Dr. Dr. Med. h.c. Gustav Schmaltz, who was a pupil of Jung, and one of the great ones in the field of analytical psychology and psychosomatic medicine. With him, and under his guidance, I did research in this field, studied the psychosomatic causes of illnesses and underwent psychoanalysis myself as a training procedure. My university certificate closed with the statement ". . . and he concerned himself brilliantly with the psychosomatic cause of diseases."

---

[10] Boeth, Jennifer: "God, Mind, and Free Will: The Scientific Evidence," An interview with Sir John Eccles, Nobel Prize winning neurophysiologist, (*Self Realization Magazine*, Vol. 55, No. 3, Summer, 1984), p. 37.

After I became a diplomate of the board of Internal Medicine in Germany, I was faced with the choice of going into private practice there, or taking a faculty position at one of the large hospitals. I decided against both, and after marrying came to the United States instead. United States law required internship and residencies which I fulfilled, including postgraduate work at the New York University, Bellevue Medical Center. After taking the state board in California, I decided to raise my family there and went into private practice. My training and thinking in terms of psychosomatics not only helped me in my therapy, but also gave me a much closer relationship with my patients.

Today, modern medicine discovers more and more that emotional stress patterns are the primary cause of diseases. Fortunately, the concepts of the great physicians of ancient times are returning today with a new name—Holistic Medicine. Body, mind, and soul are once more coming to be regarded as a unit. Now the move is to a dynamic approach which deals with the subtle electrical fields and impulses of the human entity in diagnosis and treatment.

My study of acupuncture opened new doors in my mind about the relationship of the body to these invisible but powerful human fields. In my desire to reach a deeper understanding of the human complex, I also incorporated hypnosis into my practice and began to search out the intricate worlds inside the mind.

Hypnosis has been with us for centuries, yet it has only been recognized by the medical profession in the U.S.A. in recent years. One of the pioneers in this country, William Kroger, M.D., has been one of my teachers.[11]

Many misconceptions exist regarding hypnosis, but in the hands of an experienced professional, it can promote a positive mind pattern and has been used to speed up the healing process. Hypnosis is not a sleep-state, even though the name is

---

[11] William Kroger, *Clinical and Experimental Hypnosis* (Philadelphia: J.B. Lippincott, 1963); William Kroger and William Fetzler, *Hypnosis and Behavior Modification: Imagery Conditioning* (Philadelphia: J.B. Lippincott, 1976).

taken from the Greek word *hypnos*, meaning "sleep." Rather, it is an altered state of consciousness in which increased concentration and focal awareness are experienced. Alpha rhythms are much more pronounced in hypnosis than in the sleep-state.

The depths of hypnosis depend on the personality structure, motivation, and the suggestibility of the subject, as well as on the skill and experience of the hypnotist. The best known stages of hypnosis are the light, medium, and deep trances. In light trance, complete relaxation is achieved (catalepsy of eyes and limbs); in medium trance, simple post-hypnotic suggestions may be given, personality changes, amnesia or anesthesia may occur. In deep trance, the heart rate and breathing slow down. Even major surgery is possible in this stage, because of the extent of the anesthesia.[12]

Age regression is usually performed in deep trance. The level of regression reached depends largely upon the depth of hypnosis. The patient may act out a certain period of his or her life; blocked emotional stress patterns may be released and bad choices made in the past may be turned into positive solutions. In true or complete revivication, the trance is much deeper. The patient relives a life, or a past-life, situation, with all its drama, as if it were happening in the present.[13] Such was the case with Charles Roberts. Again I want to stress that hypnosis, in itself, does not constitute therapy, but with professional therapeutic guidance, it can be invaluable in utilizing the patient's own healing capacity.[14]

Medicine, psychiatry and psychology are the proper arenas for the development of hypnosis. As a whole, it has been used only sporadically and on a limited basis by medical practitioners

[12] William Kroger, *Clinical and Experimental Hypnosis*, p. 190 reports a subtotal thyroidectomy (thyroid surgery) performed under hypnotic anesthesia. This is believed to be the first such case reported. A documentary film of this case is available from Wechsler Film Co., 802 Seward, Hollywood, CA 90038, for a rental fee. Write for details.

[13] André M. Weitzenhoffer, *General Techniques of Hypnotism* (New York: Grune & Stratton, 1957), pp. 384-385.

[14] Spiegel and Spiegel, *Trance and Treatment: Clinical Uses of Hypnosis* (New York: Basic Books, 1978), p. 20.

in this country. Barbara Brown, Ph.D. writes: "It is as if medicine fears the potential power of the mind."[15] Reports coming out of Russia, however, reveal that hypnosis is widely used throughout that country by thousands of trained psychologists. Emotional causes for various diseases are discovered which are rooted in the subconscious.[16] This therapy can help to set positive mind patterns.

It is becoming evident that the human complex that we call a man or a woman is able to heal itself on many levels. The direction has to be within. I know this. And I know that St. Luke was right when he said: "Neither shall they say, Lo here! or, Lo there! for, behold, the kingdom of God is within you."[17]

Hypnotic Regression and Past Lives— I Seek the Limits of the Soul

During my years as a medical practitioner, I have been able to observe varying stages of consciousness. My use of hypnosis has brought many of my cases of regression into what appears to be other lives beyond the scope of my patients' current life experiences. This has become a vital part of the search for the sources of human illness. I have been constantly amazed at the endless levels of human perception, and I believe that we are only beginning to open the doors of knowledge about what consciousness truly is. Theory after theory about the brain comes from science, but no one can explain adequately why the belief in an immortal soul is deeply felt in human minds.

Case histories of apparent reincarnations have piled up in my files, and I have had to address questions that arise concerning hypnotic regression. What remains after the death of the body? What is the real self? What is personality?

---

[15] Barbara Brown, *New Mind, New Body*. (New York: Bantam Books, 1974), p. 439.
[16] Henry Gris & William Dick, *The New Soviet Psychic Discoveries* (New York: Warner Books, 1978), p. 343.
[17] Luke 17: 21, King James Version of the Bible.

I am among those who believe in the rebirth of the soul, but my early training had not prepared me for this belief. Yet, somewhere in the depths of my own consciousness it seemed to be a part of me. There were many moments in my life when, without conscious thought, I reflected this conviction.

Near the end of World War II, as I assisted in the makeshift medical facilities, I found myself alone with a 17-year-old boy who had lost a leg during the retreat of the German army. The wound was infected and penicillin was not yet available to us. The infection had spread and he was in critical condition. It was Christmas Eve and he was all alone. I was sitting by his bedside, sponging his perspiring face, which was pale and childlike. Suddenly he opened his eyes. The look he gave me was one of infinite trust and an intensity I shall never forget. It was as if his soul was merging with mine. "I'm going," he said. "I know I am. Tell me—and tell me the truth: what will happen to the person I was? I am so young, there's so much I haven't learned. Will my soul remain on Earth after I'm gone? Will it take a new body? What of my family?"

I gazed out into the blue night sky. "Yes," I heard myself say. "I believe you will have a chance to learn all you need. I believe the soul will come back again and again to learn and experience."

A smile transformed my young friend's face. The soul of which we spoke slipped away quietly. I opened the window and looked out at the stars. They had smiled on me during icy nights in Russia and had taught me an impersonal peace. The same peace I felt now, looking down on the boy who had dreamed of being a man someday and who had left this lifetime without bitterness, knowing that this was not his end.

In the years to follow, my own consciousness sought expansion. Ever since my boyhood, I had been fascinated by the possibility of the existence of physical and mental disciplines which could allow glimpses of a wider reality. Paul Brunton describes the experience of his own rising consciousness at the encounter with the late Indian sage, Ramana Maharshi: "I only know that a steady river of quietness seems to be flowing near me, that a great peace is penetrating the inner reaches of my being, and that my thought-tortured brain is beginning to arrive at some rest."[18]

After the war, while still searching for an explanation of this phenomenon, I came across a book titled *Autobiography of a Yogi* by Paramahansa Yogananda, which answered many of my questions. I studied his teachings and they proved instrumental in my development.

Many years later a sequence of extraordinary occurrences took me to Southern India, where I met Sri Sathya Sai Baba, considered by many as one of the most significant spiritual leaders of modern times. The encounter with him was an event, which I cannot explain in logical terms. The experience might compare with that of Carl Friedrich von Weizsäcker, the director of the Max Planck Institute in Munich, when he knelt at the tomb of Ramana Maharshi and realized in his inner-most being: "I knew in a flash—this is it. All questions were answered. The knowledge was there. Now I was a completely different person. The one I have always been."[19]

Having gone out on such a controversial limb, I found it necessary to take a close look at alternate theories of explanation for what appear to be past life memories under hypnosis. Perhaps these memories are part of the huge picture gallery of the human subconscious which can be tapped with hypnosis. Perhaps the soul itself plays out a psychodrama concerning its own problems, under the cloak of past life recall. Often these episodes seem to bring the roots of problems into focus for the consideration of the higher mind of the patient. I have seen remarkable healing of the body and mental state after a meaningful regression.

It is commonly believed that the theory of reincarnation is an eastern concept, even though western philosophers have been pondering the possibility of evolvement through rebirth

---

[18] Paul Brunton, *Yogis*. (Wolfgang Krueger Verlag, Berlin, 1937). This book is available in English as *A Search in Secret India* (York Beach, ME: Samuel Weiser, 1970, 1985), p. 141.
[19] Carl Friedrich von Weizsäcker, *Der Garten des Menschlichen* [The Garden of Human Condition] (Munich & Vienna: Hanser Verlag, 1978), p. 595.

for centuries.[20] Recently, I found a remarkable theoretic explanation of immortality in an old Yale report:

> Since many of us have been taught that we can experience life only with the help of the body, we have come to identify life with body. Therefore, the destruction of the body seems the end. Because of a school of thought which feels that the soul-state is a state of emotion, or even one of fantasy, and that matter is the only reality, most people hesitate to leave this concept. It seems to represent logic, security, and a road to material success. Yet, philosophers and physicists alike tell us that the universe is not composed of matter only, but that other realities exist as well: and that matter is not necessarily matter at all, even though we may perceive it as such. If we assume that it is the soul which breathes life into the body, rather than the body producing life, then we must go on to conclude that the soul can exist without the body and that it existed before it entered its present home and has lived many such lives before. Modern science has found that the total sum of matter and energy is constant. If the universe preserves its lowest manifestation, namely matter, would it not follow that it preserves its highest one, namely human consciousness also?[21]

But why do we not remember past lives? I would say that it would be very confusing if we did. It may be hazardous in many ways, and hinder our process of evolution. Remembering

---

[20] For example, Plato, Voltaire, Goethe, Emerson, Nietzsche, Lessing, Carlyle, Schiller, Schopenhauer, Blake, and many others.

[21] J. Paul Williams (Prof. Mt. Holyoke College), "Belief in a Future Life," *Yale Review*, Spring, 1945, p. 283.

such experience might activate a subsystem that could affect the personality of such a person in a negative way. I am alarmed at today's trend to regress, especially if done by unqualified practitioners.

There can be uncomfortable abuses of information given irresponsibly about alleged past lives. Psychic readings of past lives are based on as yet not fully understood states of consciousness. These readings can draw from fears, hopes, or even possibly from the hidden past life remembrances of individuals.

I have looked at some of the popular books on regression. While some are written with a strong sense of ethics and scientific responsibility, others are not. Too often an individual can become fixated on some dramatic past life story planted in the mind and become obsessed with imagined relationships. This can bring terrible stress and problems to present-day relationships. And yet, it is fairly common to use past life memory as a manipulative tool. Surely, the memory of past lives is hidden from most of us for a very good reason. We do not need to remember if we have debts or links to other beings in order to work them out satisfactorily. We only need to try to act in accord with the principles of good action and loving kindness.

I do believe that regression done for the right reasons can speed up the treatment and enlarge the spectrum of human knowledge and answer questions on the interaction of ourselves and our life goals and motivations. If reincarnation is part of natural law, then we should pursue study of it with all the good means we have at our disposal.

Now I would like you to meet Charles Roberts. His case represents the incredible potential of past life regression. We will go with Charles to possible other lifetimes and meet personalities that seem to have participated in making the Charles Roberts of today. We will meet the wise one within him, who may be related to the wise personality within us all.

CHAPTER 2

THE CHARLES PUZZLE— MANY LIVES?

It is no more marvelous to be born
twice than to be born once.

—Voltaire

I met Charles Roberts in a roundabout way. In the fall of 1977, my wife was standing at a desk in a Los Angeles bookstore waiting to be helped. A customer was talking about a book she had just read, *A Matter of Immortality*, by Jess Stearn. She turned to my wife and raved about the hypnosis experience described in the book. My wife was pleased to hear this and replied that her husband had done the hypnosis Jess Stearn had used for his story of the well-known psychic, Maria Moreno. The woman bought five more copies and hurried off to tell her friends.

A very pretty young woman then approached the desk. She had listened to the conversation and asked my wife what she thought about hypnosis. She asked hesitantly if I did regressions, and if there was a very long waiting list for appointments. She went on to say that her husband had tried hypnosis for an aggressive behavior pattern which he could not understand. Perhaps hypnotic regression might be the tool to uncover a past experience—either in this life or a past life, she said.

My wife felt attracted to the appealing and vulnerable young woman and gave her my telephone number. Her husband did call my office a few weeks later and I remember chiding my wife across the breakfast table the next morning. "Since when do you send me patients from your shopping expeditions?"

A week after that I saw Charles Roberts for the first time. The man who walked into my office that day in November of 1977 was not unusual or noticeably different from any other patient that I had seen. He was 31 and carried his dark, good looks confidently. In giving his personal history, he volunteered that his father was of Scottish background and his mother was Mexican. He came from a solid working class family, grew up in Los Angeles, and quit a local college after three years because he found his engineering studies too confining. His real interest, he said, was singing, which he pursued more or less professionally.

Married in 1965, Charles needed a steady income, and took a job at a large brewery. He traveled once to Europe for four weeks in 1974, visiting Austria, Switzerland, and Germany. He has never been to England, Ireland, or China, three countries which will become important to the unfolding story.

In our first office meeting I learned that Charles needed help in controlling violent outbursts of temper, which had become a threat to his marriage and to his job. Earlier attempts at hypnosis had failed to improve his situation, and he was not sure that I could help him either, but he was willing to try.

As we began the hypnosis session, I was surprised that Charles moved immediately into a past lifetime, skipping his present life experience altogether. I would not lead a patient into such a situation, but there he was suddenly, in the midst of a tumultuous life as an Irish rebel in the year 1723, speaking in an unmistakable Irish brogue, telling me about his final agonizing hours in that life.

I now regret that I didn't tape record this first session. Any description I could give of the Irish life Charles was describing to me would only be a pale shadow of its original intensity. I have rarely been so affected by anything as by his detailed description, in deep trance, of being tortured to death on the rack by British soldiers. The rage in his voice was chilling.

My wife wrote in her personal notes about my response to that session: "Eugene arrived home looking shaken. He did not speak for a few hours. When he did, he only mentioned that Charles had been taken straight into what appeared to be a past life. Witnessing the hopelessness of this lifetime as well as the indescribable agony ending it, Eugene wondered if he would ever again want to hypnotize him."

But Charles himself wanted to continue with hypnosis. He felt that whatever had happened in our first meeting had eased some of his emotional turmoil. Even his wife, almost at once, began to notice a change for the better.

And so I continued working with him, being careful for a time not to move into the Irish life, but rather to direct his attention to other lives that his subconscious might wish to explore.[1] In the weeks to follow I met several of Charles' earlier personalities: as Aliena, a 17-year-old Mexican-Indian girl (no date given); as Chang Lu, an overseer of a priest's home in China in 1422; as Jonathan Mikter, a German farmer in the wooded mountains near a place he called Wildeman (no date given); as Octavian, a Roman Soldier in the year A.D. 23; and as Ranta, a scientist in Atlantis.

The most interesting lives of all were a life as Colin O'Brian, a rebel in Ireland, and a life as James Stewart, a banker in 19th century England. These lifetimes were recent enough to be examined for accuracy, something I was able to do the following year, when I traveled to England with my wife, Maya, and daughter, Nicole, and then on to Ireland, intent on investigating the things that James Stewart and Colin O'Brian had told me of their lives. The complete transcripts of the sessions with James Stewart and later sessions with Colin O'Brian are given here, along with the intriguing trail of discovery I followed in England and Ireland.[2]

---

[1] Whenever I had Charles go through the time of torture again in Ireland, I made sure that he would look at it unemotionally and objectively without experiencing the agony of torture.

[2] We were unable to locate a place called Wildeman on our German map. A year later, while doing research on German Health Spas, I happened upon a place called Wildemann. The place is isolated and little known. It is a village in the Oberharz Mountains, surrounded by deep pine forests. The area is located in Thueringen, which then belonged to East Germany. Wildemann is a village of 1400 inhabitants and is used as a spa.

Hypnotic Regression
Irish Life

July 3, 1977

Q: What is your name?

A: Cook. Cowell—Cowen?

Q: Can you spell it for me, please?

A: O-B-r-i-a-n.

Q: Is that your full name?

A: Colin. C-o-l-i-n. Colin O'Brian.

Q: How old are you now?

A: I am 19 years of age, Sir.

Q: Where are you now?

A: Near the barn.

Q: Are you in a village? Do you know the name of the place?

A: Donegal.

Q: Can you spell it?

A: D-o-n-e-g-a-l.

Q: Where is that?

A: Ireland.

Q: Near Dublin?

A: Oh—quite a way from it!

Q: Is it on the same side of the country as Dublin?

A: It be the odd side.[3]

Q: The other side?

A: Yes

Q: What are you doing right now?

A: Hiding from the bloody British in a barn.

Q: In a barn? Why do you say the "bloody British?"

A: Well, they've been hunting me for days.

Q: Why are they looking for you?

A: Inasmuch as I have killed a number of their soldiers, you might say that I am high on their priority list.

Q: What is your profession?

A: I am a farmer by trade—but who can make a living under these conditions . . .

Q: So, what do you do?

A: My duty!

Q: And what is that?

A: Killing the bloody British!

---

[3] "Odd side" is a typical Irish expression referring to the "other side."

Q: Nineteen years old and killing the British?

A: I am not alone in this.

Q: Who is with you now?

A: Many—we must rid this area of the British. They are taking our livelihood. They are starving us! This cannot continue! We must be rid of them, and soon. They have brought a blight onto this land. We will not be whole—we shan't have anything until they are gone. And I will do all in my power to see to that.

Q: How do you fight?

A: We would be citizen soldiers. We are organized in all the towns—from Armagh to Dublin.

Q: Are you one of the leaders in this warfare?

A: I am.

Q: So very young, only 19, yet you were already a leader?

A: What do you mean—I was?

Q: When were you born?

A: 1704.

Q: Where did you go to school?

A: I've never been to school in my life!

Q: Are your parents alive?

A: They have been dead for years. Poor devils. Mom worked herself to death—she was only 34.

Q: Why did they have to work so hard? Were they slaves?

A: Trying to keep their own place. Trying to hold onto their own place, with taxes what they are.

Q: How old was your father when he died?

A: A young man. He was 38 years old when he was killed.

Q: Any brothers or sisters?

A: One brother is still alive—the British chased him away years ago. Ain't heard nothing from him since . . .

Q: You were a rebel . . .

A: I *AM* a rebel! I am one of the rebellious![4]

Q: Are you well known?

A: (Chuckles) . . . I daresay . . . (chuckles again) . . . I slept in every house in town. But I bring much trouble to them that take me in . . . much trouble. And they have enough troubles already.

Q: Can you tell me the name of an important battle?

A: Ah—man, these are skirmishes. Skirmishes. And each one is important.

Q: Do you know the name of your leader?

---

[4] When I asked in the past tense, "You were a rebel?" Charles in a deep trance, corrected me, his voice rising as if he felt insulted, "I *am* a rebel!" This shows us again his emotional involvement in the past time frame and past personality as a rebel. In other words, in revivication, the past becomes the present.

A: Well—there are many . . . There's Sullivan, Sully. He comes . . .

Q: Comes and brings you orders? Is there a headquarters?

A: Dublin. There's Tully, Andy, Andrew Tully.

Q: One of your leaders?

A: Aye—there's Michael also . . .

Q: Think of a major encounter now. Can you give me a year?

A: 1723.

Q: Did you win?

A: At this point in time, unfortunately, we have lost many, many fine men—and women—and children, more than we gained. But we will win. We shall win. God is in our favor, He is on our side, don't you see? Man, we must be rid of these bloody British.

Q: How long have you been fighting?

A: This has been going on for many years, man. For many, many years. We seek independence from the British. All we ask is to be left alone. I am a peaceful man. But I cannot tolerate these conditions any longer! My father was killed by the British, my brothers have been killed by the British, I have no doubt that I will be killed by the British, but I must continue this quest.

Q: How many years have you been fighting them?

A: I have been fighting them all my life, Sir.

Q: Have you ever been wounded?

A: I have been, many times.

Q: In jail?

A: Many times.

Q: Where was that?

A: This year it was the stockades.

Q: What parts of your body were wounded?

A: I've been shot three times, Sir. Twice in me arm, and once in the leg. Not to mention the countless beatings . . .

Q: What about diseases?

A: We have infection. Constant plagues we cannot get rid of. The British don't care how sick we get. They probably wish we'd all die—would save them a round of ammunition or two . . .

Q: How long were you in jail?

A: The longest they left me in would be three months. They couldn't prove anything yet—till this time.

Q: What do they want to find out from you?

A: Oh, first of all, the location of our central meetings. Also, from where we get our orders, how many organizers we have, who they are, they shan't be finding out from me . . .

Q: Do you give many speeches?

A: Don't take many "speeches" to get these men in steam, man!

Q: No?

A: Not under these conditions. They'll not leave us alone. They tax us until there's nothing left. They treat us worse than animals. They spit on us in the street. They kick us when we walk by. They take every bit of self-respect from a man, strip him of it. They take our women at will . . . They brutalize our children. I will not stand for it any longer and I will kill every Goddamn one of them, this I swear!

Q: Are you married?

A: Ah, no. I have no time for that, man. No time for that.

Q: Did you stay mainly in this area?

A: I have traveled all the way to Dublin, organizing the small towns, convincing men that they must come and bear arms.

Q: What are your weapons?

A: Rifles, swords, pitchforks, stones, whatever we get our hands on we use. We are poorly equipped. And farmers are not meant to be warriors. It's nary impossible to make them into fighting men—but it shall be done. I may not live to see it, but God knows it will be done. And we will be rid of the bloody British!

Q: Do you believe in God, do you go to church?

A: I believe in God, yes. But I've not set foot into a church for many a year, and God knows I will not . . .

Q: Why do you hate the church?

A: All they tell us is cooperate with the British! They preach that this is the way of God! I curse the day they have taken over our churches.

Q: Tell me something about the color green . . .

A: Aye, man! Me word . . . I have an armband, green armband. It means that I am one of the fighting. I cannot show it when I walk the streets, but I wear it constantly, under me coat.

Q: Where are you living now?

A: I have lived under this house of mine for quite some time now.

Q: In the cellar?

A: No, man. Under the house. Dugout.

Q: How do you eat?

A: Food is brought by friends. If the British knew where I am, I'd be in the stockades right now. I'm fortunate that I managed to keep alive. God knows I need my air to kill these bloody British.

Q: Breathe in and out slowly now. I want you to tell me how you died. You are not emotional about this anymore. You are dead now. You look down and you can describe to me how you died . . . How old were you?

A: 20.

Q: Can you tell me how you died?

A: I was put on a machine, that stretched my limbs, my arms, my head, and one by one, first my left arm was pulled out, then my right arm. The left leg (breathing heavily), the left knee, and then the other . . . and I was still conscious . . . they threw water on my face . . . and then, with a sword, they stabbed me until I died . . . I died . . .

Q: What happened to your body? Were you buried?

A: They threw my body in the river outside.[5]

Q: You were not buried then?

A: No.

Q: Relax now. Breathe slowly in and out. Your thoughts are drifting away now, you feel peaceful now, very rested. Slowly you are coming back to your present life. When I have counted to fifteen, you will begin to wake up. One . . . two . . . three . . . .

---

[5] After leaving the Irish life, the subject no longer spoke in an Irish brogue.

Hypnotic Regression Northampton

November 29, 1977

Q: What is your name?

A: James.[6]

Q: Your surname?

A: Stewart.

Q: Stewart?

A: Stewart.

Q: Where do you live now?

A: York. Yorkshire . . . Yorkshire Road.

Q: What number?

A: 17 Yorkshire.

Q: Where is that place?

A: Northampton.

Q: Where is that?

A: Britain.

Q: How far is it from London?

---

[6] James was pronounced with a strong inflection, so that spelled phonetically, the name sounded like "Ja-y-mes."

A: Three day journey.

Q: Three what?

A: Three day journey.

Q: When were you born?

A: Believe it was in 1801.

Q: Have you a middle name?

A: Edward.

Q: Do you recall your father's name?

A: William. William Edward. William Edward.

Q: Your mother's name?

A: Alice? I believe, Alice.

Q: What does your father do?

A: He owns a bank.

Q: Owns a bank?

A: Yes.

Q: And what do you do?

A: I go to school.

Q: Do you know the name of your school?

A: Gray . . . Cra . . . Kreton, Craiton, great . . .

Q: Can you spell it?

A: Creighton.

Q: How old are you now?

A: I am 12 years old.

Q: How long have you gone to this school?

A: I also went to the Draidon School.

Q: Do you live at home?

A: I live at school now, too far.

Q: Is your school in Northampton?

A: Outskirts of town. Too far to walk.

Q: What did you do before you went to school?

A: I stayed in the house most of the time.

Q: Did you have a large house?

A: Yes, very.

Q: What is your mother like?

A: Well, she is very small. She is quite fragile, rather sickly. Mum is always sick.

Q: Does she stay in bed?

A: Yes.

Q: Who is her doctor?

A: Dr. Williamson.

Q: When you were little, were you sick a lot too?

A: Yes.

Q: What was wrong with you?

A: Colds.

Q: Cold?

A: Always!

Q: What medicine did you get for your cold?

A: Some stuff to drink.

Q: Did Dr. Williamson treat you, too?

A: Williams.

Q: Well, now you are at school. When did you leave school?

A: I have not left yet . . .

Q: You are now 16 years of age. Do you still go to school?

A: Yes!!!

Q: Now you are 17. Are you still in school?

A: No.

Q: What are you doing right now?

A: I have taken leave of my education for a short time to try to pursue some form of pleasant diversion from all those academics. Studying! I am rather tired of studying.

Q: So? What are you doing?

A: I am preparing for a trip into London.

Q: Have you been there before?

A: When I was small.

Q: What kind of transportation do you have?

A: Well, we have our own horses and carriage.

Q: How many horses?

A: For a long journey such as this one, we always use four horses.

Q: How long does the trip take?

A: Normally, three days. We do not wish to push the animals unless it is absolutely necessary.

Q: Where do you stay overnight?

A: Wayside Inn.

Q: Do you recall the names of those inns?

A: Wayside Inn. Can't recall names. Small little village outside of town.

Q: And where will your next stop be?

A: All depends on our horses here. We may continue on.

Q: Okay. Now I will count to three and you are now in London. One, two, three. You are in London. What do you see?

A: Oh, marvelous! Marvelous city!

Q: Where are you staying?

A: Stay at the all-man's-club my father belongs to here.[7]

Q: Is that the name? It must be a famous club?

A: I don't know if you'd call it famous or not . . .

Q: What is its name?

A: Land . . . there's land in the name—can't make out second . . .

Q: Try spelling it . . .

A: Land. L-a-n-d, lan, london . . . The London Club.

Q: What street is it on?

A: Don't know.

Q: Do you know other places?

A: I will be exploring as the days progress.

Q: What do you do?

A: As I told you before, I am here for some pleasant diversion.

Q: Like what?

A: Oh, I'll take in a theatre, of course, do a bit of shopping and spending and—look at the ladies—that of course, will come first.

---

[7] What sounded like "All Man's Club" could also have been interpreted as "Almack's Club."

Q: Do you have a girlfriend?

A: No. I'm not one with the ladies.

Q: Do you go to bordellos?

A: (chuckles) Yes.

Q: For sex?

A: Of course.

Q: Do you have a special person there? Someone you really like?

A: I like variety, thank you.

Q: Who is ruling England right now?

A: Let's see . . . we have a king amongst us, I know that. Edward comes to mind. But right now it is Victoria.

Q: What profession do you want to follow?

A: Oh, my father wishes me to pursue a banking career, but I don't think that will be my cup of tea. I don't know what I'm going to do.

Q: Do you know the name of your father's bank? Its location?

A: Canterby . . .

Q: Canterby street, or Canterby bank?

A: Street. Savings bank.

Q: Can you walk there from your house?

A: About two blocks away from there.

Q: Now we count from one to three and you are at the bank. One, two, three. You are in the bank. You are working here, in what capacity?

A: I am an assistant teller—and I hate it!

Q: Do you have friends here?

A: No! I cannot stand these people. I'll get out of here as soon as possible.

Q: Is that what you did?

A: I beg your pardon?

Q: I count from one to three now, and you are no longer in the bank. One, two, three. You are 25 years of age. What are you doing now?

A: I'm back in London.

Q: Doing what?

A: Nothing.

Q: 25 years old and doing nothing?

A: Nothing.

Q: Is your father supporting you?

A: Indeed.

Q: Didn't you have fights with your father about that? That you are not working?

A: Yes, of course, we did.

Q: So, you left home?

A: Just for a while.

Q: I will now count from one to three; you are 30 years old. One, two, three. 30 years old. What are you doing now?

A: I am back in the bank.

Q: In what capacity are you working there now?

A: I have taken over for my deceased father.

Q: When did he die? How old was he?

A: He was 64 years old.

Q: Were you with him? How did he die?

A: Yes. A strain on his heart, overworked himself, poor man.

Q: And now you are the banker?

A: Well, I refuse to put myself into the same position my father was in. I have no use for that type of life. I have hired an employee to oversee the bank's workings.

Q: Are you well liked?

A: Oh, of course not.

Q: Of course not?

A: No, not at all. I can't stand those people.

Q: Did you serve in the army?

A: I was able to, let us say, buy myself out. My father saw to that. Who in the world wants to go to India! My heavens!

Q: Why India?

A: 'Cause that is where many of my colleagues ended up that joined the service.

Q: I see. Now I will again count from one to three, and you will be 40. One, two, three. You are 40 years old. What are you doing?

A: I have become more involved in this bank. I've diversified into investments.

Q: Do you make a lot of money?

A: Yes, property, land . . .

Q: Do you have a hobby?

A: No.

Q: What do you do with the money?

A: Reinvest.

Q: Are you married?

A: No, can't seem to find a lady right for me.

Q: How's that?

A: You must understand; I am a man of great wealth and any of these ladies would take me for my money, and I can't allow that to happen.

Q: Are you a religious man? Do you believe in God?

A: No. Not at all.

Q: I want you to go forward in time now, to the time you die. How old are you?

A: I believe, believe I am 59 years old.

Q: Are you very sick?

A: Yes.

Q: Do you know what is wrong with you?

A: No . . . those stupid doctors can't tell me.

Q: Do you have a fever? Do you feel hot?

A: Cold. Always so cold.

Q: And is the same doctor taking care of you, Dr. Williams?

A: Oh, heavens no! He died years ago.

Q: Who is treating you now?

A: Dr. Lavitt.

Q: Is he giving you injections? Pills?

A: No, he gives me these herbs to drink.

Q: Does it help you?

A: No.

Q: Are you dying. Do you know the date of your death? The season?

A: It was cold . . . was winter. '61 I believe. 1861.

Q: Where are you buried?

A: I am buried in a small cemetery.

Q: The name?

A: It's a church.

Q: A Protestant church? Do you know the name?

A: Anglican church. Saint James.[8]

Q: St. James?

A: Yes, Saint James.

Q: Would you say that your life has been a happy one?

A: No, not at all.

Q: Do you recall how you felt at the moment of your death?

A: There was a tremendous amount of fear within me at the time of my death.

Q: Why was that?

A: I was not a religious man, Sir.

Q: Did you believe in life after death?

A: None whatsoever.

Q: Did you experience that your soul remained alive after death?

---

[8] Charles pronounced the words "Saint James" with a heavy British accent, so that James sounded like "Ja-y-mes." It is possible that he said "Saint Giles."

A: After I left my body I was aware, first of all, that nobody gave much of a damn that I had left my existence. Second, I was frightened and did not wish to go towards the light which was beckoning. I went the opposite way, for I did not want to leave the area of the life I had been living. I soon realized that I was out of my body and could no longer communicate with the living. Terrifying experience. I roamed about the town, I stayed in the house, now no way to make contact. I can see them quite clearly. I have my own body, Sir. It is a body to me. I look quite well. I'm in my youth.

Q: How long did you remain in this soul state?

A: It is rather difficult to time the days. I became weary of my existence, realizing that I could not communicate with the living. Obviously, there was more to life and death than I had believed. I decided to follow this individual who called himself my friend, and we spoke for a long time. He reassured me that there was nothing to fear, that this was a transitory period.

Q: In your soul-state, did you find your parents again?

A: I had seen my mother briefly as I made the transition. My father came to visit me later. He was not a religious person. He was always too preoccupied with work. But we felt that we would reincarnate again to improve our relationship.

Q: Later on, did you meet others?

A: Oh yes, many. School friends . . . Andrew . . . I recognized them. Many, many . . .

Q: Okay. I want you to relax now. When you want to wake up you will wake up into the life of your present incarnation. I will count from one to three and you will open your eyes and feel very refreshed. You will wake up to the life of Charles. One, two, three.

We Search for
James Stewart and Colin O'Brian

It was the summer of 1978. My wife and daughter weren't eager to leave London on a gray and drizzly day to chase after phantoms from Charles' past. We took the train for Northampton, some seventy miles to the north. This wasn't the kind of family holiday we had dreamed about, and we could not make any firm plans because we had no idea where our investigations would lead us. The weather had its effect on us as well, and from my first glimpse of the dreariness of Northampton, I questioned that anything interesting awaited us there. I never felt that it would be easy, or that we would simply take a cab to number 17 Yorkshire Road, find a talkative descendent of the Stewart family, and be told that everything Charles had said under hypnosis was true.

Northampton is a cattle and leather town with the feel of a small industrial center. It was crowded this particular day—with a leather convention. We went to several hotels before finding one that could give us a room. As quickly as we could, we hired a cab to take us to the Town Hall by way of St. James' Church. We knew from our brief research in London that there was a St. James' just as Charles had said. The sun was starting to come out from behind an overcast sky as we drew up to the church. I knew immediately that it was the wrong one. It was a stone building, no more than sixty or eighty years old, and there was no cemetery around it, just a part which was fenced and locked. The church was closed as well.

Our second disappointment was that the Town Hall was closed. It would reopen after lunch hour, so we dismissed the taxi and started to walk around Northampton. We were restless and eager to find something. Maya had enough faith in her ESP to think that we might be drawn to some of the places Charles had described. It was a long walk through the town, past leather shops, a leathercraft museum, and a place where a cattle market was being held. Near the museum, at the end of town, we passed a very large and elaborate church called All Saints. Even though it had a graveyard, I knew it was not

Charles' church. So we continued on a short way to a green grassy place that looked like a beautiful park. Settled in the midst of all this natural beauty was St. Giles Church, at least several hundred years old, and it had a graveyard next to it. This corresponded to the picture that Charles had given us of his neighborhood church and cemetery.

As we started back to visit the Town Hall, we passed a mortuary. Nicole insisted that we go in. Sometimes mortuaries have old records and she felt somebody here might be helpful in our search. At first we were a disappointment to the proprietor, as we did not have a death in the family and only wanted information. One of the employees said he would be happy to take a little time to help us out. We asked directions to Yorkshire Road, but he said there wasn't one, only a York Road. We asked if there could be another St. James church and cemetery. His answer was an intriguing one: There is only one St. James. Since it does not have its own cemetery, the people who die in that parish used to be buried in St. Giles. When Charles had said "St. James," he had pronounced it "St. Jaymes" and it sounded very much like St. Giles. When Charles said "Jaymes," could he have really been saying St. Giles?

We left the mortuary as quickly as good manners allowed and went back to St. Giles Church. It could have been the fashionable church of 150 years ago. We entered the part that was surrounded by a high iron fence, and found that the gravestones that had been there had been removed and placed artistically in groups to one side, no longer marking any of the graves. There had been many old inscriptions, and we looked at all of them. By now it was raining and we were wading in the water, frustrated that the names on the stones were so worn by time and the elements. The church was still closed.

We set out to find York Road, and discovered it was just around the corner from St. Giles, as Charles had told us his home had been in relation to the church. The houses on the street were very old, some of them old enough to have been Charles'. We felt that this had once been a part of the well-to-do neighborhood of old Northampton. The area around number 17 had been torn down and replaced by brick buildings. But the surrounding houses were of a type described in the hypnosis sessions.

It began to feel right to me and to Maya, as well. We took a cab to the Town Hall, and here again were frustrated to find that their records extended only fifty years back, and no further. The undertaker seemed our best source of information, and so we returned to the mortuary. Several hearses passed us going in and the place was buzzing with activity. We said to the undertaker, "Business must be flourishing," and he replied, "Oh yes, they just keep dropping dead right and left at this time of the year. Unfortunately, I'm not the owner. I just work here." He referred us to the vicar of St. Giles for more information on the parish records, and volunteered to telephone to the vicarage on our behalf.

We made a serious mistake in strategy at this point by neglecting to anticipate any negative reactions to our quest. The vicar was on vacation, it seemed, and our undertaker friend spoke to the assistant vicar, explaining why we were here and that I did research on reincarnation. The man on the other end of the line shut up like a clam. He refused to call the vicar. I felt he might change his mind if we paid a personal call on him. I must have seemed like an agent of the devil, because when we arrived at the assistant vicar's house, his very pregnant wife would not let us come inside. She just closed the door right in our faces, saying "No, no, no!"

I regretted that we were so foolishly honest and felt sick inside at the probability that I would be denied access to the very records I had traveled so far to see. We had been tantalized by just enough clues to guarantee our obstinance, and I decided to climb the church hierarchy until I found someone who would help me. Later, I looked at this episode in our trip as a test of my faith in the proper working out of events. However, after calling the bishop's office and being told that he, too, was on vacation, I began to feel that perhaps I wasn't supposed to be here in Northampton after all.

We returned once more to our mortician friend and asked bleakly for any further advice he could give us. "You have to go the Abbey," he said. "They keep records for all of Canterbury Province."

Delapre Abbey, centuries ago, was once a nunnery, and is now a secular public establishment. Situated in a large green park outside the city, it looked to be the perfect place to house historical records. We had with us a list of potentially verifiable facts about the Northampton life of James Stewart, if such a man really existed.

We were looking for a banker whose possible date of death was 1861. He died of pneumonia and was buried either in St. James, or in the other church nearby, St. Giles. Both churches were near his house. In his childhood, he was attended by Dr. Williams, and at his death by a Dr. Levitt.[9] His father's bank was two blocks from home. As a child he was a student at Great Creighton School, an institution for boys.

With the help of the kindly historians in the abbey we found two directories. Slater's Commercial Directory of 1862, and Mercer & Crocker's Historical Directory of 1871. Almost immediately I found a Great Creaton School listed under academies and schools. It was located just outside of town in the village of Spratton. (During a later session Charles had said that he was a boarding student and that it was too far to walk to his school. He also mentioned another school which sounded like "Dryton," or "Dreyton" which was about three blocks from his home.) A second school in the directories, Dryden School, was located a few blocks from York Road. The school was founded in 1710, and the building now houses the leathercraft museum which we had seen on our first day in Northampton. Great Creaton School no longer exists.

We found reference to the Savings Bank on St. Giles square, close to York Road. It, too, no longer existed. So far, Charles' geography was accurate, if we allowed the York Road of present day to be Yorkshire Road. The second school and the bank were within the distance he described. Charles said the bank was on Canterbury Street, but street names had been changed in the past one hundred and fifty years, and we could find no complete records of 19th century street names. There is no

---

[9] We transcribed notes based on what we heard. Some spellings of names may vary, and we have left the variations in the text.

Canterbury Street today, and we found no one named James Stewart who had been a banker in that time.

Looking under the directory of surgeons, we found a Dr. William Williams, who was still living in 1862. A Dr. Flewitt was also listed. Allowing for the distortion that often comes with names recalled in hypnosis, we may have found Charles' Dr. William Williams and Dr. Levitt.

We began searching through masses of baptismal and death records from the parish of St. Giles. There we found a Dr. Kerr Williams recorded as having been buried in St. Giles cemetery in 1791. Dr. Flewitt died in 1871 and is also buried at St. Giles.

The most suspenseful moment at the abbey came when we turned to page 068 G of the St. Giles parish death registry and found that a man named John Stewart had died of pneumonia on June 4, 1861.

We had our man Stewart who had died of pneumonia though his first name was John instead of James. Yet, no other Stewart had died there in 1861. The names Stewart, Stuart and Steward are rare in this part of England.

By now we were sure that the mind of Charles somehow had access to information about the layout and inhabitants of Northampton in the mid-19th century. Since Charles had never traveled to England, it seemed ridiculous to credit him with extensive research that he could have only done on location in Northampton, itself. If he had studied the history of the city, why didn't he give us the correct names of the doctors and provide us with a genuine banker?

What we were examining in the abbey were obscure records, endless lists of names in small print, lists unavailable unless one traveled to England. Northampton was a town of about 50,000 people a century ago. I can't imagine the odds of Charles Roberts guessing correctly the things he told us. I was satisfied that, although I couldn't make sense of everything, Charles was familiar with a life lived in that city at that time. I was intrigued by the fact that Northampton was known for its breweries in the 19th century, and that Charles, in his present incarnation, was working for a large brewery.

Back in London we looked into the lifestyle of old London to verify points of James Stewart's rather hedonistic social life. We located a club called the London Club. Charles had mentioned a London Club. This club had opened its doors in 1768. Charles had also referred to an All Man's Club, but in listening to the tape again, I believe that he could have been saying Almack's Club. Both were prominent men's clubs in their day. One could join the Almack's Club only by election. This was a select membership with an annual subscription. It was a club which fostered cultural endeavors, poetry readings, etc., as well as gambling. Before the long reign of Queen Victoria, England was ruled by King Edward. Charles had mentioned both monarchs.

Encouraged by these findings, and buoyed by the number of hits and near hits with James Stewart, we decided to go on to Ireland to see what we could find on the life of Colin O'Brian of Donegal.

In Ireland we had more difficulty than in England. Colin O'Brian had lived two hundred and fifty years ago, and had not been a notable personage. Because of the innumerable skirmishes between Irish rebels and the English over the years, records had been lost. However, Colin's recollection of the social, economic, and political situation in Ireland was true to the history that we researched.

Charles, in his first meeting with me, had mentioned that long ago he had had a strange vision of wearing something green on his sleeve. He had never connected it with anything; since his personal background was not Irish, he had no reason to realize that green is the patriotic color of that land. In hypnotic sessions Colin O'Brian spoke proudly of wearing his green armband.

So, we had very little proof that Colin really had existed. Yet there were many points of accuracy concerning history in his accounts, especially the painful intensity of Irish sentiments toward the British, and the use of the infamous rack as an instrument of torture. Colin's home county of Donegal in those days was a seaport, market post town, parish, and head of a union. It had three streets, 177 houses, and a marketplace. These

were the days when Catholic worship was prohibited and atten-
dance at the Anglican service was compulsory—the days of
the "priest hunts" and of gang-enforced tax collections. The
lavish extravagances of the rulers were paid with monies
extracted from the oppressed. Although it was apparently not
a common name, there were O'Brian's in county Donegal. We
did find an Edmund O'Bryan of Duntarson Fawthen Parish 2,
1665, County Donegal, in the Hearth Money Roll. Soon after
that date, records were destroyed as mentioned earlier.

CHAPTER 3

BETWEEN LIVES—
THE FRIEND ON THE OTHER SIDE

Man is a universe, in which the higher conditions
can influence the lower if only they are allowed to
do so.

—Isha Schwaller de Lubicz
The Opening of the Way

If there was anything consistent in these life memories of
Charles, it was his meetings with a "friend and teacher" after
death. James Stewart of Northampton was frightened of death.
The Mexican girl and the Chinese man accepted and understood death. Colin O'Brian was filled with rage as he died and
felt bitterness toward church rulership and its doctrines. The
German farmer had no apparent belief, one way or the other.
Yet all encountered a nameless companion as they made the
transition from this life to the next.

I was familiar with the medical studies of deathbed visions,
where patients have described a kind of spiritual being or figure of light who lovingly awaited them and reviewed their
lives with them.[1] In the case of Dr. George Ritchie, he himself
experienced clinical death and wrote about his life-changing
encounter with a spiritual teacher whom he called Jesus, during
the time that his body was presumed to be dead.

I vividly recall a conversation with the famed and
respected Dr. Paul Niehans. It took place in Clarens,
Switzerland, while we were walking down the street to his lab-
oratory. We had been talking about the fetal cell therapy he was

---

[1] See the published works of Drs. Raymond Moody, George Ritchie, Karlis
Osis, and Michael Sabom. Also see Kenneth Ring, *Heading Toward Omega*
(New York: Quill, Morrow, 1984).

so involved in. I had done quite a bit of research in this field, and now we were talking about consciousness. Consciousness in matter, in spirit, in stones, in cells, in life, in death, and beyond. As he stopped to collect his thoughts, his gaze traveled far away, and as he stood there in the afternoon sun, his features bore an uncanny resemblance to another man, known and loved for his modesty and understatement. This man was Emperor Wilhelm II, to whom Professor Niehans was related. His blue eyes came penetratingly back to my face. "There was a man," he said, "who was technically dead. Later he was brought back by means of heart massage, artificial respiration, etc., and he told us that while he was 'dead' he was moving through a tunnel. Moving freely and without any breathing difficulties. It was dark in the tunnel and he perceived a light at the far end. He moved closer to it, and then, as he said, 'someone seized me by the neck and I woke up.' This reminds me," Niehans continued, "of a story my father once told me. A similar story. He was working at the time in Bern, as chief surgeon. His patient went into a coma and was considered dead. But he also was revived, and he told of walking down a dim tunnel toward a bright light. He perceived other shadows as he walked along. Coming closer to the light, he woke up." Niehans smiled. "Dying can be difficult. But I am sure that death is easy. And life . . ." his gaze became distant again, ". . . life is an art."

We went on to consider the opinion of Carl Jung, who maintained that part of our psyche very likely continues beyond death, impervious to time and space. Jung quoted cases of total shock, where the cerebral cortex had ceased to function and where vivid dream experiences had occurred despite a total lack of consciousness.

Of course, we reasoned, these people had not been truly dead. What of the dreams just before waking up? What of the light one may perceive through the orbs just before opening the eyes after a heavy sleep?

Many years have passed since my talk with Dr. Niehans. Today the controversy regarding body, mind, and soul has taken on fierce proportions and has divided professionals in the field of medicine and psychology into two camps. There are those who believe in the reality of the split consciousness and who use this concept in a number of ways: to aid analysis, to aid healing, to investigate the various energies of mind and body, and the many energy fields connected with the organs.

Andrija Puharich, a neurologist with a sparkling mind, describes, in one of his books, a mobile center of consciousness which, he believes, exists independent of the physical body.[2]

The other group, by and large the greater, maintains that there is no valid evidence, as yet, for such survival, that all experiences presented so far can be explained in medical and psychological terminology. Nevertheless, mainline medical journals are now reporting on the subject which would have been shunned at the time of my conversation with Niehans. A symposium on near death experiences appeared only recently in the *Journal of Nervous and Mental Diseases*. This debate over the possibility of a split of consciousness represents a revolution in a rigid thinking process. All we can lose in this revolution, I believe, are chains.

I agree with Johann Wolfgang von Goethe when he writes: "I am certain that the soul lives on and will continue through eternity. It is like the sun which, to our eyes, appears to set in the evening but, in reality, has gone to shed its light everywhere."[3]

As I studied the transcripts of Charles' past life sessions, I began to suspect that he was describing not only the same "shining being" mentioned by Moody and the others, but something else. There seemed to exist an entity who had a continuing and very personal interest in Charles' spiritual progress.

Here is the end of the first session with James Stewart in Northampton. He speaks of death:

Q: Do you remember your burial?

---

[2] Andrija Puharich, *Beyond Telepathy* (Garden City, NY: Doubleday, 1962), see Chapter 7, the mobile center of consciousness, independent of a living physical body, pp. 83-92.

[3] George B. Brownwell, *Reincarnation* (Santa Barbara, CA: The Aquarian Ministry, n.d.), p. 150.

A: At the time of my death there was a tremendous amount of fear within me.

Q: Why?

A: I was not a religious man, Sir.

Q: Did you believe in life after death?

A: None whatsoever.

Q: Did you experience that your soul was alive after death? Can you tell me anything about soul life?

A: As I left my body, I was acutely aware that no one gave much of a damn that I had left my existence. Second, I was very much frightened and I did not want to go to the light that was beckoning me to come. I went the opposite way, for I did not want to leave my area of life where I was living. I knew shortly after that I was indeed out of my body, and could not communicate with the living, terrifying experience. I must say that I roamed about the town, I stayed in the house, I traveled about. The caretakers were living in the house now, no way to make contact. I can see them quite clearly.

Q: How long did you stay in this soul life after death?

A: It is rather difficult to time the days. I became weary of my existence, realizing that communication with the living was impossible, that there was obviously something more to death than I had believed. I decided to follow this individual who called himself my friend, and we spoke for a long time and had many discussions on the subject of life after death. He reassured me that it was nothing to be frightened of, that it is a transitory period.

That was Charles' first mention of this "friend" on the other side. In two later Northampton regressions, he again mentions his friend. When Charles relived the life as a German farmer, I asked him whether he could see any people waiting for him on the other side. He said, "yes."

Q: Who is waiting for you?

A: A bright light and I am being told not to be frightened and I will be taken care of.

Q: Who tells you that?

A: A friend.

Q: What is his name?

A: I do not know.

James Stewart and the German farmer both spoke of the "light" to which they were drawn. But the nameless friend seemed to be apart from this light. The following are more excerpts from other lives:

Life as a Mexican girl:

Q: After you died, what happened to your soul?

A: I was met by my wonderful friend. I do not know him by his name. He is ageless. He is not in all my lives. In most. He helped me in spiritual progress.

Q: What is the teaching of your friend?

A: Immediately after death, the transition, we would speak of my experiences of that lifetime, and the lessons that were learned and also of the karma that was produced, the mistakes that we made.

Life in 15th century China:

Q: Can you tell me, after you died, what happened to your soul?

A: My body was burned.

Q: Could you see that?

A: I had no desire to stay . . . (the tape is not clear for a few words here) . . . to my friend and teacher.

Q: Is this like someone, like a guide, who is with you in all your lives?

A: He has been with me in previous lives.

Q: As a friend or a guide?

A: As a teacher.

Q: Not in physical body?

A: No.

Q: Spiritual body?

A: Yes.

In another session with the Chinese life:

A: After my death in that lifetime, I met with my friend and teacher.

Q: Do you know his name? This friend's name?

A: We do not use names.

contents, and Jung's followers were afraid that it would hurt his standing. So the book was attributed to Basilides, a gnostic of Alexandria: ". . . Alexandria, 'the city where the East toucheth the West.'"[6]

After Jung's death, his authorship was revealed. Jung had mentioned Philemon in his memoirs. He also had sketched Philemon. The sketch appears in his *Red Book,* and also in *Memories, Dreams, Reflections.*

Philemon seemed quite real to Jung and he enjoyed their conversations and shared a fathomless depth of understanding as they walked together in the garden. Jung stated: "Philemon represented a force which was not myself. . . . For I observed clearly that it was he who spoke, not I."[7]

---

[6] Serrano, Miguel, *C.G. Jung and Hermann Hesse: A Record of Two Friendships.* (New York: Schocken Books, 1966), pp. 93-94.
[7] C.G. Jung, *Memories, Dreams, Reflections,* recorded and edited by Aniela Jaffé, translated from German by Richard and Clara Winston (New York: Pantheon, 1961), p. 183.

CHAPTER 4

THE BIRTH OF YAN SU LU

That which wakes the Spirit in you is an appeal
from the Master of your soul.

—Isha Schwaller de Lubicz
The Opening of the Way

As I was preparing for the next session with Charles, I thought
about how strange our situation had grown to be. I was anxious
for him to arrive and I had questions that demanded answers.
If there really were a separate entity who acted as Charles'
teacher, had this friendship formed in one life, or in many
together? What had they been to each other? Had they known
each other at all in physical form? Did this friend influence his
steps in this life?

Charles was late. He would be tired. Perhaps I should
reschedule his session. Even though his former aggressive
behavior was changed, he was still a touchy patient, easily hurt.

I was right. When he arrived he was tired. He slumped in
the chair and closed his eyes. I looked at him for a while. He
had a handsome face, dark eyes, a sensitive mouth and a halo
of black curly hair. Charles' Latin background had gifted him
with a beautiful singing voice. I began talking about music and
he started feeling better. We would proceed with the session.

"Who are you, friend of Charles?" I asked. "Would you be
willing to come and join us here? If you would like to tell me
about your friendship with Charles, perhaps it would be of
help to him . . ."

By now, Charles was in a hypnotic trance. He was stretched
out in the chair. Suddenly, he sat very straight with his head
high. He seemed much thinner and older. He folded his hands.
His face took on an Oriental cast and his facial muscles started

to twitch. He seemed to be under a tremendous strain. His mouth tried to form words, but at first nothing came through. Then a voice came, barely audible, then stronger. It was a mature voice of a different timbre, scratchy yet soft.

"I am Yan Su Lu." I was not sure if I heard right. I asked again, "Who are you?" The answer came: "Yan Su Lu is my name. I am the one Charles calls his friend and teacher. There are many of us, but I have been helping Charles with his adjustment whenever he made transition from this earth life." The voice had a Chinese accent. There seemed to be a smile in this voice, and impersonal happiness.

As my conversation with Yan Su Lu continued, I learned that he wanted to teach Eastern philosophy to the Western world. I had not expected anything like this. I had not even taped this first session. I brought Charles out of hypnosis and asked him if he remembered anything which had happened during that session. He denied it. I asked him if he would be willing to continue with these sessions. He was not very eager to do this at first, but finally gave in when I told him that I, myself, was very interested in this Yan Su Lu phenomenon, and wanted to study it by all means.

So, my acquaintance with Yan Su Lu started, and our journey began into this newly discovered part of Charles' consciousness. What follows is the transcript of our first recorded conversation in which Yan Su Lu introduces himself and describes himself and his relationship to Charles. The date was February 28, 1978.

Session One

Q: I want to make contact with your guide and teacher.

A: Yan Su Lu.

Q: Yan Su Lu is your name?

A: Yes.

Q: What nationality are you?

A: I chose to assume the personality of my last incarnation, which was of Chinese nationality.

Q: When did you live?

A: My last voyage on this plane was in the year 1232.

Q: Where did you live then?

A: In China.

Q: Can you tell us about that life?

A: I lived only a short time in that incarnation as there was only one lesson left for me to accomplish and within a span of fourteen of your years, I had completed my earth living, which is not to say that I have not yet to return, for there is still much to be done; but it will not be a life as you know yours to be at this time.

Q: Do you now work as a spiritual teacher on the other side to help us here?

A: At this moment, yes, it is our intention to assume the teaching and direction of Charles.

Q: What is your relationship to Charles?

A: You would call me at this time, friend and teacher.

Q: And how are you able to teach him?

A: It is not entirely easy with this entity because he is given to have many, many directions. If he would allow himself more time in the meditative areas, we would be better able to utilize his energies and to heighten his spiritual awareness. But since we cannot be with him at all times, we do as much as possible in allowing him to contact us when he desires, through sporadic meditation. We also utilize the channels of his subconscious mind, dropping our thoughts to him in the period of sleep, which is greatly important as a tool for us, on this side, to channel our thoughts and ideas into his mind.

Q: During sleep, do you approach Charles in his dream state?

A: Not as much in dream state, as in sleep state.

Q: What is a sleep state?

A: One where the energies would be almost, but not completely shut down, so that little energy emanates from body and from mind. It is at this time that the subconscious mind becomes most perceptive and acutely aware of new ideas coming from this side.

Q: In other words, you say that in the sleep state the five senses are shut off, and there is actually more energy available for the subconscious mind to make contact?

A: Yes.

Q: Can you tell me the difference between the subconscious state, and the super-conscious state?

A: These definitions you use do not apply here; but, from what I can gather from your mind, what you are asking in sense is, where does the spiritual consciousness reside, is that so?

Q: Yes, because I think the spiritual consciousness is the same as the super-consciousness or the divine consciousness.

A: There are many names people use, but for our purposes I would use the terminology of spiritual consciousness, God consciousness. This resides not in the brain area, but within the spiritual and psychic centers in the bodies.

Q: Can you tell us what kind of body you have now?

A: It would be most difficult to explain, for you have not yet seen this energy form that I am at this moment.

Q: Can you describe it?

A: Let us say, if you or Charles would avail yourselves of the potential that is within you, you would, by using the psychic eye, perceive a radiant energy form shaped in a manner not unlike your physical body, but as a more constantly moving form—how could I describe this to you . . .

Q: Is it a ball?

A: No. It is round, it is not a sphere.

Q: Is it changing shape all the time?

A: It is constantly moving. As I have brought myself down to this point, to allow communication through Charles, there has been constant change within my energy form. If I were not to communicate in this manner, but rather if you would start to see me, utilizing your psychic senses, then you would see a smaller form than your physical body is, one that would be transparent, but yet, not completely.

Q: Does this body have any weight?

A: It would be weightless.

Q: We would like to know, Yan Su Lu, why you choose this particular time to communicate with Charles? Is it possible that the life regressions we performed on Charles facilitated your communication with him, or is it that our energies enable you to communicate so strongly now?

A: There are no accidents. The meetings which took place between you, Dorothy, and Charles, in beginning were planned long time ago. It was a pattern which had to happen. The impressions upon Charles, Dorothy, and yourself were strong enough so that each one of you understood the necessity of this communication.

Q: Thank you, Yan Su Lu. I would like to ask . . .

A: May I interrupt you? Excuse me. I hope you understand; I do not mean that this was ordained by some outside influence. It was not. Each and every one of you has ordained his or her life up to this point.

Q: What was your relationship to former lives of Charles?

A: I have been one of many teachers that have surrounded Charles in previous incarnations.

Q: Have you ever been Charles' teacher in physical form, or were you always a soul teacher?

A: A soul teacher.

Q: On the other plane?

A: Yes.

Q: When he entered the soul state between his physical lives?

A: That is true.

Q: Were you always with him when he died?

A: When he made the transition from the physical to the spiritual, I along with others, have been there with him many times.

Q: When you say "others," can you tell me more? Are they teachers, too, or are they relatives.

A: These are teachers that I speak of. You must understand that each and every one of you has more than one teacher.

Q: More than one?

A: Yes. One attracts teachers according to one's need for spiritual help.

Q: Could you tell me what Charles' best abilities are in this present life, and what he should do professionally.

A: We are only interested in his spiritual growth. What he wishes to do on the physical plane is entirely up to him.

Q: Thank you. Were you helping Charles in former lifetimes?

A: We have been with Charles before, but not as close as we are in this lifetime. This is first lifetime that Charles has been awakened enough to receive as a channel messages such as these. Before, we have been with him in spirit and, indeed, we have communicated with him telepathically, but never in this manner.

Q: Thank you. Do you know Charles' future fate?

A: It is not necessary to speak of his fate at this time, but yes, it is known.

Q: Are you an independent entity which comes through Charles utilizing his vocal chords?

A: That is so, yes.

Q: Yan Su Lu, you seem to be a spiritual teacher. Have you been in any of your own lifetimes, involved in such work?

A: There were many, many lifetimes involved in spiritual teaching. The last one would have been my last incarnation in China.

Q: In what capacity?

A: I was able to utilize my spiritual abilities to the extent that "phenomena" as you would call it, such as healing, clairvoyance, telepathy, all these things were available to me in my human form. And being the son of a priest in that town, it was quite easy for me to be totally dedicated to my work.

Q: Do you dwell now in a so-called astral body?

A: There are many words for this in your language. One cannot clearly understand it completely until one can observe. Since "astral" is a word that people are becoming used to hearing, we will use that word, that description.

Q: Do you remember all your lifetimes in physical bodies, and do you remember all your soul states?

A: As one progresses to the point of evolution where incarnations are no longer necessary, all awareness is given to you. By this I mean, total recall of all lifetimes one has lived. Whereas this may seem to you to be overwhelming, believe me, it is not. Thoughts can be stored forever. There is no limitation to your thoughts. By thinking, you do remember. In particular, you recall the most important aspects of those lives. You are able to trace the karmic threads which exist from one lifetime to another. Progress of soul is by that time of evolution obviously known, and so recall of lives becomes a rather simple matter.

Q: It would then be easy for you, for instance, to tell us of your life on earth before the Chinese life?

A: This incarnation was short in life span. I made the transition in your year of 1215. I was at that time 12 years old, a male body, but also a female body. In other words, I had reached the point where balance was permeating my entire existence. Female and male qualities. I was not a normal human being. I had left that point of life before. This was a brief physical existence to allow myself one last opportunity to understand the balance that is so necessary for all of us at one point in time. My existence was not in an area where I lived with normal people, but in the mountains where I was, for the most part of my life, isolated. There was not need for close relationships as one knows them between mother and father. These souls that bore me were mission souls, brought here specifically to assist me in this incarnation. And so I was devoted in my entire life to utilizing the spiritual teachings given to me at such an early age.

By the time I was 1 year old, I had already perfected much of what your average 10- or 12- year-old child would in his lifetime. These are rather simple matters in terms of evolution. In this respect my life was not one of normality, but one of necessity concerning my spiritual growth. I had chosen Asian life for that was yet one lifetime I had not been incarnated into very often. The souls which were chosen to bear me had other lessons to experience in that nationality. Therefore, this was shown to me as the best possible of all choices.

Q: If you were to compare yourself with other spiritual teachers, what degree of evolvement have you achieved?

A: This is difficult question to answer inasmuch as the ego could possib misinterpret what I have to say. If I was a far evolved spiritual teacher, I trust that would smack of an ego which was greatly distorted. And yet, if I were to say to you that I was low on the ladder of spiritual evolution, I trust that confidence and faith might wither. Let us say I'm somewhere in the middle.

Q: Have you been, or will you be reborn on other planets or solar systems?

A: As it is with myself, it shall be with all of you. Existence is not specifically for this planet. Once you have reached the point of growth and balance here, there are other experiences to be gained, lessons to be learned in other galaxies. This is an infinite universe. There are infinite ways of growth and experience. There is no stagnation in this universe. One does not evolve then and cease. It would be impossible. The Father did not intend it to be this way. We are always learning, growing, always.

It had been a long and tiring session. Charles showed signs of fatigue. Before I dehypnotized him, I asked Yan Su Lu if he would always guide Charles. His answer came without hesitation.

A: As long as he continues on his path of spiritual quest, we will be assisting him as much as is possible. But his desire must be strong, and it must be continued.

Q: Will meditation improve this desire?

A: Yes, greatly.

Afterward, Charles showed no interest in listening to a playback of the session we had just recorded. I had already decided that until I understood more about the nature of this Yan Su Lu phenomenon, I would rather not confuse Charles with the details of it. It was sufficient at the time for him to know that we had apparently tapped into a subpersonality of his that acted as a friend and teacher.

CHAPTER 5

THE CONVERSATIONS CONTINUE . . . .

We are all at the threshold of a new spiritual
epoch . . . the longing for security in an age of inse-
curity. It is from the need and distress that new
forms of existence arise and not from idealistic
requirements or mere wishes.

—C.G. Jung
Psychology and Religion

Yan Su Lu appeared to have an absolute belief in life after death.
After all, he claimed to be on the other side, and he should
know in that case. I had to ask myself many questions concerning his teachings about other dimensions. From what
source did these teachings arise? I remembered what Plato had
written: "All souls do not easily recall the things of the other
world; they are seen through a glass dimly. And there are few
who, going to the images, behold in them the realities and these
only with difficulty."

Is there a common pool of human subconscious knowledge from which Charles and every other human being can
draw material about other states of being and consciousness?
Was I speaking sometimes to that higher part of Charles' mind
that was linked with universal truths, and at other times merely
tapping ideas stored in his mind remembered from his brief
study of philosophy in college?

Was Charles, as is often suggested about hypnotized subjects, wanting to tell me something that I would like to hear
and so drawing on the picture gallery of human ideas to find
answers? Or, was Yan Su Lu a separate being as he claimed
to be?

If he was a separate being, did all of his ideas come through clearly, or was the mind of Charles a filter which let in some light and blocked other areas by the quality of his own personal self? It seemed as though the friend/teacher figure was benevolent. It did not carry much that wasn't of good quality.

I do not believe it is good to regard any being, unseen, or even a better part of an individual self, as infallible. However, Yan Su Lu often made good sense. I decided that whoever the real Yan Su Lu was, he was in touch with a stream of universal knowledge, and I hoped that such knowledge would be of real service to Charles within himself. After all, that was supposed to be the true purpose of the connection between Charles and his teacher.

Our second session was a continuation of the first in general tone, with my Chinese friend explaining more about his own evolution as a wisdom figure and his relationship to Charles. He still insisted that he was an entirely separate entity from Charles, and had had his own many incarnations on this planet. He was more than willing to go into careful detail about the way in which he used Charles' mind and nervous system to speak to me.

Session Two: May 17, 1978

A: Good evening.

Q: Good evening.

A: It is indeed our most humble pleasure to be here this evening and to assist in whatever way we may. While we are on the subject of Charles, it might be proper to advise as to how channel is used. As you are well aware, not all can be channels. There must be certain amount of evolution upon spiritual path at one lifetime or another.[1] Although all humans have

---

[1] Readers should note that Yan Su Lu spoke in his own way, often skipping articles and pronouns. His text has been taken from our tapes and has not been edited.

potential, it is not always accessible for that lifetime. In Charles' case, since he had in previous lifetimes been involved in spiritual matters, he is able to utilize these abilities in this lifetime, and we in turn, are able to utilize them also.

The point of entrance is centered behind the neck. After that point of contact is made, we are able to take over his nervous system, thereby utilizing control of vocal chords, facial expressions, use of arms and legs, etc. This can only happen with the permission of the channel, for you all have free will, and unless you openly and freely allow spirits to enter, they cannot. In cases of possession by negative entities, the individual either physically or psychologically has given up his or her free will, allowing possession to take place. But in the cases of those like Charles, who wish to use his ability in a positive way, it cannot be done without permission. May we proceed now?

Q: Yes. When and where did your relationship with Charles begin? Was it on Earth, was it in another galaxy, or was it in the soul state?

A: The relationship between Charles and myself began much like any teacher-pupil relationship. What has transpired between him and myself has also transpired between you and your own teachers. To give specific point in time would be an impossibility, for we are not talking in terms of specific dates on physical lifetimes when we are speaking of this relationship.

I shall now concern myself with Charles and myself. Our relationship has taken place, in your terminology, to use the word "centuries," and it has its beginning, if you must call it that, at a level you would not have here. In other words, it did not begin on this planet or in a vibratory energy that exists here. This began while he was experiencing other forms of life in another sphere of living. We have not been together always with each preceding incarnation, for each lifetime requires certain experiences to be met. Therefore, it was not necessary for me to be with him during all incarnations. This is universal law. This is what happens between every living soul and his teacher.

Q: Does this mean that the relationship between you and Charles began in the soul state?

A: Relationship began before Charles had incarnated in the physical life on this planet.

Q: Did this take place in another galaxy, or was he in energy form? Were you both energy forms at that time?

A: I had completed my evolution in that sphere of life where Charles had begun his. Therefore, it was my voluntary choice to direct him through that sphere of existence. It was and continues to be a learning process for him. He is not through, nor are all of you completely through with the experiences that one must have in order to evolve on the spiritual path in these other spheres of life.

Q: Who were you at that time? Were you already a guide on the other side, or were you both entities in that galaxy at that moment?

A: If you wish to use the word "guide," then you could because I was voluntarily giving him direction, helping him and making it easier for him in this new form of existence.

Q: Who was Charles at that time? Did he have a physical body?

A: His form of energy was not within a physical body. It was a combination of spiritual and mental existence. There are many forms of energy to be experienced by all of us, this being only one.

Q: Has there ever been any karma between you and Charles?

A: No, there has not. We have not lived together on this planet at any time. When Charles began his sojourn here on this planet, he had other teachers and brothers to assist him with the different experiences. I, in my own time and within my own evolutionary plan, when I was in this planet's state, I was also able, depending upon what experiences have to be met, to best utilize my own abilities in directing him so that the experiences could be learned as quickly as possible without interruption. This is easier said than accomplished. As you know, we all possess free will and in these matters we will many times come to Fall and not allow these spiritual directions and teachings to take place. But, nonetheless, we on this side do all we possibly can to eliminate any of these, let us say, detours.

Q: Yan Su Lu, what is the basis for the soul attraction between you and Charles? Did he select you as his teacher, or did you select him as your student?

A: This was done voluntarily on both parts. We both have choice. It is most difficult to break down into simple terminology, but it would be best said that we had met, we both understood that he, Charles, would need assistance from one who had evolved and had experienced what he must now experience. I, in my sojourn of spiritual evolution also realized that it would be possible for me to lend assistance in God's plan. There is constant assistance given from soul to soul, energy to energy. It was entirely our choice. But you understand it is not really a matter of choice when we are speaking at that level, for the love that is transmitted from soul to soul also brings with it automatic understanding of what must be done. It is not a matter of two souls, let us say, sitting at a table and discussing whether or not they would like to enter a relationship. It does not happen this way.

Q: Is it then a form of magnetic thought?

A: Indeed.

Q: Is there any way of clarifying exactly what a teacher can do for an individual when you obviously cannot actually speak with him? What type of things did you do with Charles in order to help him before you actually could communicate with him?

A: When direct communication is not possible between both sides, communication is given telepathically, and when one is in the sleep state. It is during these times that we impart as much energy as possible in order to assist in the problems that surround the soul at that time.

Q: And that involves . . .

A: This involves telepathic messages as to perhaps reading material that one might pick up accidentally; you would wish to call it accidentally, but we would tell you that it was our impression that led you to that material.

Q: Is it possible for a teacher to deter his own evolution in order to remain exclusively with one pupil?

A: There are instances when a soul assigns itself to a particular incarnate being because of various problems that have arisen. This is the teacher's choice. It is done with a great deal of love. The teacher fully knows that because he has volunteered on this mission, he is putting off his own evolution and his own experiences. But, because so much love is involved here, he does not mind. Yes, there are teachers who would remain. And I might add that this happens many, many times, it is not unusual at all.

Q: Would a teacher take on the sicknesses of others as some yogis claim to do?

A: This a teacher would not do. They would allow themselves to continue the relationship with the incarnate soul, but never to take away the problems.

I found this a satisfactory answer and I ended the session.

As clear as Yan Su Lu's answers usually were, I noticed that sometimes he referred to himself in the singular and sometimes in the plural. I therefore asked him once again to explain, which he did without hesitation.

A: When I say "our," it is, as I have mentioned before, because the knowledge that will be forthcoming is not entirely always my own. As Charles is channel, I, too, become channel. Knowledge of other brothers and teachers flows through me and through Charles. I am always in contact with them, and they with me. So, therefore, what shall be presented at these meetings will not come only from me. You may use the title, the name of Yan Su Lu for simplification in your material.

When pressed for further explanation, Yan Su Lu continued:

A: In order to assure this communication I must tell you that there are others who assist myself and Charles in this. I, myself, would not be able to enter into Charles' body were it not for our brothers that lend their energy here and create a funnel of energy, a positive energy, that enables me to continue the contact and lets us put Charles at this point (here, Charles gestures to show the relative distance with his hands) and myself at this point. It would be impossible for Charles at this point to come up here. So other brothers intercede in the middle and throw out their energies, lifting Charles' vibration to a meeting place where I am then able to make proper contact.

Q: Yan Su Lu, what happens to Charles' consciousness once proper contact is made? Is his consciousness completely set aside?

A: No, not completely. He has asked from the beginning when we first met and communicated with him that this should not happen, and of course we appreciate his concern. But for the most part, it is set aside during the course of the meeting, for it would become rather difficult for him to sustain consciousness and at the same time allow me to utilize his nervous system and allowing the correct interpretation of the energy that comes through. His consciousness is not clear most of the time, it comes and goes.

Q: What degree of recall has Charles of your dialogue with us?

A: Depending on whether he is able to focus in on what we are speaking of, only he will know.

Q: Is Charles capable of exercising his will in altering the words that you use?

A: When he becomes conscious of this conversation, he will find it most difficult to do this, yet it could be done. But what would transpire would be his will versus the tremendous amount of energy that is coming through him, and he will begin to speak incoherently, with much stuttering. At that point we would desist from attempting communication.

Q: What vocabulary do you use, is it Charles' or yours?

A: It must be the vocabulary of Charles. In order to facilitate this connection we must rely completely on his knowledge of the language and the proper words that would be used. At times, when you see hesitation, it is because we are searching through his mind for word that best describes what we wish to use.

Session Three: May 4, 1978

Session three deviated dramatically from the first two in that Yan Su Lu explained to us that he was unable to make proper contact with Charles. He emphasized that Charles must be sufficiently rested for these meetings to take place, and that in future he would instruct him telepathically.[2]

I include this session to show the reader that contact was not always possible, and Yan Su Lu himself would terminate the session.

A: Good evening.

---

[2] In future meetings Charles would generally notify us if he felt too tired to participate in a session.

Q: Good evening, Yan Su Lu.

A: (Long pause) It will not be possible to continue this evening, as Charles is not able to make proper connection. It is most difficult and we do not wish to absorb more of his energies. We had instructed him telepathically this day that it would not be wise to attempt the communications this evening. In future, he will have to understand that when these thoughts come to him they must be heeded. These meetings can only be accomplished by having all of you imparting necessary energies to the channel. The channel most of all, must have energies sufficiently high so that we can make proper contact. You would be well advised that although you find it necessary in your own time and schedule to insist that these proceedings take place, we must advise you that what happens is always for reason. Time, your time, is not important.

We cannot continue for this evening. Please remember for future reference that Charles must be sufficiently rested or this will not take place again. And he will know if and when that should occur. You will listen, he must listen to us in order to alleviate any discomfort among all of you. We will meet again when you find it proper.

Good night, God bless you all.

CHAPTER 6

YAN SU LU
ANSWERS GENERAL QUESTIONS

The blossom vanishes of itself as the fruit grows. So
will your lower self vanish as the divine grows in
you.

—Ramakrishna

By mid-1978 my meetings with Charles were no longer part of
an ongoing therapeutic process. Our roles were shifting now.
Charles found himself able to go into a trance state alone and
bring forth the Yan Su Lu personality without my involvement
as a hypnotist.[1] Each time after Charles had hypnotized himself,
a process which took a couple of minutes, he would put his
palms together in a typical prayer position and greet me. From
this time on he decided when a session should end, at which
time he graciously bid me "good evening" with a slight bow
and then slowly lowered his hands to his knees. The facial
expression of Yan Su Lu changed until it was once again
Charles'. I thus became observer and questioner.

Our evening sessions proceeded this way for almost two
years, as did the wide ranging teachings that flowed from
Charles. As I listened, I recognized many of Yan Su Lu's themes
and viewpoints from esoteric literature, and from my encoun-
ters with spiritual teachers. However, much remained which
gave me an expanded view of Yan Su Lu's universe, a world
which I had never glimpsed before.

Another development of interest was that Charles had
decided to seek a divorce from his wife. The fact that Yan Su Lu
came through him with a very stable emotional tone didn't
seem to translate easily to Charles' everyday life, although it

---

[1] I taught Charles to hypnotize himself.

was clear he was going through some kind of prolonged process of life evaluation.

Still, I met with Yan Su Lu in those evening sessions in my office, wondering all the time where Charles' mind left off and Yan Su Lu's began, and especially, if both were part of a larger whole.

In this chapter I have drawn from my files some of the material expounded by my Chinese philosopher friend because it might interest the general reader.

On Universal Wisdom, and Seeking the Teacher Within

Q: What topic do you want to discuss this evening?

A: I would at this time talk about the abilities that lie within each and every human as they inhabit this planet. There is no soul that breathes life into a body that is devoid of the Godliness and God's power within him. These words are certainly not new. They have been spoken by many before me and will be spoken by many others after.

It is within your time that simplicity has lost much of its meaning. Words of love and faith, honesty, morality, have become rather nebulous. We are now seeing a society that is base and condoning a level of consciousness which is further from the truth. The Father did not mean for His truth to be mystical, to be secretive, for the Father has said: "Look into Thee. All answers are within." We must understand that the Father, in his love for us, would never have borne us here under abstract, secretive and nonunderstandable means. Our life was to be one of knowledge. But knowledge that was easily understood. Confusion has arisen through interpretation of this knowledge.

Through all these years we have seen much evolution in spiritual matters, but of course, not enough. I speak, and will continue to speak in manner that will be understood by Western philosophy, since it is my understanding that this material you are compiling will be centered here in your country. There is much that could be said about other philosophies. One might ask about the conflict between philosophies, but we shall see in proceeding, the conflict is only in interpretation. The difference between truth as the Father gave it to you and us, and the truth as mankind would hold it to be at this point, is the ego in mankind, man's need to have a way of life which is better than that of his fellow man.

Nevertheless, you have entered into an age of enlightenment. However, mankind does not evolve rapidly, and progress as you would like, it will not be quickly done. But we do see spiritual evolution here. Again, you must understand I am speaking of your Western world.

All are blessed with spiritual potential which is hidden in most, for they refuse to accept and utilize the power that is within them. Mankind as it exists at this moment, utilizes so little of the God power that is within. You might ask, how does one communicate with this dimension? Again, meditation. Silence. It is essential that the person understands the need for silence, and the need to be able to be alone with his thoughts. Only in such times can he utilize his energies to communicate with the Father within. By communicating in this manner, all answers to all problems are available.

For those who cannot yet seek this manner of communication, you have with you individuals that have evolved, that have allowed their psychic abilities to open. These people are here for the purpose to guide, direct, advise, as best they can.

But this is limited, for you then assume that the person with these abilities would interpret your pattern entirely correctly. This is not always possible, inasmuch as the power utilized from within is still governed from without. Also, as long as the individual seeking guidance maintains a path away from spirit, he would have problems trusting his interpretation.

You are now living in time when the words of extrasensory perception, clairvoyance, and meditation have brought upon themselves new meanings. Many people are following these ideas. I would warn that they follow not complete truth, but only small portion of truth, and discretion is advised.

Would you ask questions at this time?

Q: What is the best path to acquire knowledge and to find out true self?

A: In order to find true self, this can only happen through analysis of one's emotions, ideals, philosophies. We must, in searching for true self, always understand that within you lie all answers. And while these answers may not be forthcoming as quickly as you would like, nonetheless, they will come. But you must seek the council of the Father within.

You must understand that while it is good and needful to utilize your meditative periods for answers to these questions, in order to receive more than partial answer, you must be able to deal quite honestly with your own imperfections in body and mind.

For what answer may come to you as to how to solve problems, solutions cannot take place without your understanding that ego must be removed. Fears must be removed. Answers to questions will not always seem the easier manner in which to solve problem. At times, it would be painful and inconvenient. But these times and these inconveniences are entirely of your own choice.

Your own free will has brought you to this point with all its imperfections. Therefore, when answer is needed, answer is always given. But because ego has not removed itself, answer is not solution. Clean thy house mentally in order for answer to be able to work on solution.

Q: I glanced at the note pad on my lap; "Ask Yan Su Lu the necessity for a personal guru." I wanted to throw Yan Su Lu into a discussion on this subject because so many people around the world are seeking a guru, a spiritual teacher.

They vary from the seeker in India whose own religious tradition predisposes him to feel that there is somewhere, his own guru, to the unsettled American whose complex society weighs too heavily on him or her. In both East and West these searching people can find many a self-appointed teacher willing to deal with their problems, often for a substantial price in money or services.

I have investigated quite a few of these gurus of both cultures and seldom encountered the supportive spiritual common sense that should be the hallmark of a true teacher. The guru market is overcrowded. Promises of bliss, unusual powers, or a lifting of one's own karma (results of action) vie for the attention of the hopeful students. In many people there lies the deep but undirected hope for enlightenment, for some viewpoint that will help make sense out of existence. But the search is smothered beneath the ceremonies, meditation techniques, chantings, or lectures of the multitude of teachers. The shrewdness and coolness of these so-called teachers who cash in on the urgent need for understanding which now flows in many minds, is one of the saddest spectacles of our time. It was for this reason I asked Yan Su Lu to speak about gurus:

Many feel that it is necessary to find a physical guru or master to guide and support them. What is your opinion on this?

A: Using your terminology, you must understand that each and every one of us have our teachers, our gurus, if you may. They are always with us; the sole purpose is to direct the soul onto a positive spiritual path.[2]

In many cases this becomes almost impossible. In many individuals, the conscious mind has so overtaken the spiritual thoughts the soul would send out, that it becomes an impossible task. But nonetheless, teachers are and remain with us at all times. If one feels the need for direction, for advice, for learning, from whom they consider physical master or teacher, then this is good, but only after carefully evaluating the teachings of said master. For there are infinite paths to the Father and not all

---

[2] I was immediately reminded of the words of the Indian teacher, Sri Sathya Sai Baba: "He who tells you of this all pervasive God is the real guru, not he who promised you salvation. Salvation, if you place a purse at his feet. Do not be misled by such a worldly man full of greed and egoism. Pray to God to illuminate your mind, awaken your intelligence and be your guru. He will surely guide you aright, from the altar of your own heart." (From *Sadhana, The Inward Path*, Brindavan, Bangalore, India: Sri Sathya Sai Education and Publication Foundation, nd, p. 201.)

teachings and philosophies would ring true to each and every one of us at our particular time of evolution.

Q: I next asked Yan Su Lu the following question: "What is meant by self-realization?"

A: Self-realization is the understanding of what the soul would tell oneself. In other words, self-realization can be achieved in moments of meditation. Through silent meditation one can communicate with one's own life force, one's own soul, and at this time the problems that the conscious mind has experienced can then quite possibly be alleviated by the knowledge that would be coming from within, and also at these times self-realization would pertain to the acknowledgment of the Father, the God-force that is within us and through this acknowledgment and this communication, one's own spiritual direction would be enhanced and greatly developed, let us say.

Q: I had to think for a moment, because the words of my late friend and teacher, Professor Schmaltz came suddenly to mind: "Behind the consciousness in the dark realm of the soul, the unconsciousness, there exists something which thinks and meditates independently, acts upon the consciousness, and together with it 'makes the truth.'"[3] In pursuing this thought further, I asked Yan Su Lu to explain the difference between full self-realization and divine vision.

A: One who is self-realized in his spiritual knowledge is one who is living that spiritual knowledge; he is indeed one with knowledge. He has become that, he has communicated with that inner part of himself, the God-self, the soul, and he has grown. One with divine vision may be able to see those spiritual

---

[3] Gustav Schmaltz, *"Das Machen der Wahrheit im eigenen Herzen" (Augustinus) und die dialektische Funktion des Unbewussten im Individuationsprozess [Meditation in Religion und Psychotherapie]* (Stuttgart, 1958), p. 95. Dr. Schmaltz was one of my teachers. This book has not been published in English. A translation of the title would be: The "making" of the truth in one's own heart (Augustinus) and the dialectic function of the unconscious in the process of individuation.

things, but seeing does not necessarily mean that he is living these spiritual things.

Q: Can you explain to us the concept of the Trinity—Father, Son and Holy Ghost?

A: This can be simply described as being the modern explanation for the three aspects of man; the spiritual, the mental, and the physical, for on this planet we have these three aspects of life. We do not necessarily exist in quite this manner in other realms of existence, but only here on Earth.

Q: Is your teaching, Yan Su Lu, in conflict with Christianity?

A: To a degree, as mankind has chosen to explain Christianity. If we are speaking of the teaching of the great Master Jesus, of course not. Any teacher who would be in disagreement with a master would not call himself a teacher. What we would have disagreement with would be the individual religions that have given birth to misconcepts.[4] But as for the original teachings of the Master, they are all nothing but loving truth.

Q: Is there a guideline as to how we should conduct our lives on this planet?

A: In as much as every soul comes into this life with different karma and different life patterns, the one specific that can be given here would be the ability to love, unselfishly, for with love, unselfish love, comes understanding and tolerance and open-mindedness. Much can be learned from this emotion,

---

[4] According to Jung, the main function of formalized religion is to protect people against the direct experience of God. See Stanislav Grof, *The Adventure of Self-Discovery* (Albany: State University Press of New York, 1988), p. 269. And Gandhi said: "I believe that all the great religions of the world are true more or less. I say more or less, because I believe that everything the human hand touches by reason of the very fact that human beings are imperfect, becomes imperfect." See R. K. Prabhu, *Mohan-Mala: A Gandhi Rosary* (Ammedabad, India: Navajivan Publishing House, 1949), p. 36.

from this word, love, but it is easier to say than to live, quite obviously, for the turmoil that exists in the world is living example of how far people have strayed from this love. More than that, to discover one's own life plan, there must be an understanding and a belief in the Father, and with this belief, comes the knowledge that the Father resides in all of us.

Q: Is there anything we can do to neutralize the negativity and violence that prevails throughout the world?

A: Your body is the temple of your Father; the temple of your spiritual soul. This is where you reside and this is where you have your peace and your harmony. Untouched by the outside world and events. For you must understand your own purpose in life, deciding to live it in a most positive, loving, tolerant, understanding manner. And if you can achieve this, then it does not matter what happens in the events outside yourself. The most important event that can happen is within your own self.

Q: Yan Su Lu's answer reminded me of one given by the great Indian sage, Sri Bagavan Maharshi when a disciple asked:

H: Master, can I help the world?

Bh: Help yourself and you will help the world.

H: I wish to help the world. Shall I not be helpful?

Bh: Yes, helping yourself you help the world. You are in the world, you are the world. You are not different from the world, nor is the world different from you.[5]

---

[5] Arthur Osborn, *Ramana Maharshi and the Path of Self-Knowledge* (York Beach, ME: Samuel Weiser, 1973), p. 99.

On Meditation, Time and Eternity

Q: We have talked many times about meditation during our sessions, and you advocate meditation as a path toward God. Are there also other ways, or is meditation the only way?

A: One cannot speak highly enough of the use of meditation for spiritual growth. How else can we expect to evolve unless we make our own personal communion with Father? Without communication with Father, evolvement takes much longer. But once the realization takes place, then the awakening of our spiritual consciousness enhances our path, our steps upward in evolution. Of course, once an individual chooses a life of honesty, morality, and integrity, then without realizing it, or holding spiritual concepts, this individual is upon the spiritual path.

But how much faster would the individual evolve if he or she would take a small moment of time to communicate with the Father, and learn what a precious gift He has given us, the gift of life, the most beautiful, loving gift of life; and with this life, how to best evolve into the being that the Father meant us to be. This, my brothers and sisters, is why we are here, to evolve into this beautiful person that is inside of all of us. Let us bring that individual out, expose him to the world and then see the beauty that will surround us.

Q: What do you mean by meditation?

A: Meditation means different things to different people. But whatever it means to the individual, whether it be prayer, conscious thought directed to Father, thought directed to one's own self, it is one way, one direction to understand what one's life is all about.

Q: Yan Su Lu, in your dimension, do you have an awareness of time whatsoever?

A: In our state, let us say, in the etheric state, there is no such word as time. This exists solely for the benefit of mankind within mankind's own dimension. It is not necessary here. One does not think of time. We do not view life in terms of time, for there is no tomorrow, there is no today. There is always, always now, and now is forever. I do not wish to sound as if I am avoiding the answer, but we must bear in mind that on the etheric level, even with souls who have come from the physical to the etheric rather quickly, these souls, in time, as they begin to lose their Earth personality also begin to lose sense of time. It does not exist here at all.[6]

On the Vibration of Names and Soul Patterns, or Predestination

Q: What does the name Yan Su Lu mean?

A: What does the name Eugene Jussek mean?

Q: A vibratory thing?

A: Indeed, as most names are. They are given before the life process is begun. Every letter has its own vibratory rate which coincides with the vibration and pattern on which that individual proceeds through his lifetime.

There comes a time, when changes regarding the name can be made. The changes which occur during one's lifetime may, at the right time, necessitate a change of name in order to have the proper vibration. It is not absolutely necessary but indeed much better, since—as one can understand—changes from within would also bring changes from without.

Q: Does the word "soul" have a special vibratory significance?

A: The word "soul," in your vocabulary, brings with it the vibratory rate most useful in regard to this energy. In other

---

[6] In this context referral could be made to Stanislav Grof, *The Adventure of Self-Discovery* (State University of New York Press, 1988), Chapter 1, Dimensions of Consciousness: New Cartography of the Human Psyche.

words, if the word "soul" was repeated over and over in your language, it would carry a high vibratory rate, for it does pertain to that aspect of the body which is called the God-self.

The God-self, that part of every human which has within either him or her the life force which the Father gives to us all, we call this life force the soul. There are, of course, other names in other languages for it, but we wish to stay here with the English terminology.

Now then, the word "soul" was chosen because it brings with it that which means "God's life force" in the vibratory sense. This soul is energy force, it is unseen, but without it in the physical body, life would not be sustained for very long. I say "for very long," for at the time of fetal development the soul has not yet inhabited the body.[7]

Soul brings with it all patterns through which that individual will learn during his lifetime. The soul recognizes the inequities its personality may encounter regarding consciousness and free will. Nevertheless, it tries to remain the individual's motivating, governing force, inspiring and directing his or her life.

No karma can dictate that a soul should come as a negative individual. We are not born this way. It is a learned process. Negativity dismisses the soul's influence and karmic pattern. It allows willfulness to override all direction from within. In essence, I am saying that all souls come with positive guidance. No one is meant to bring negative experience unto one's self or onto others; no one is meant to do harm to another, morally, spiritually, or physically. This happens only because ego insists and prevents the spirit-soul to direct.

Q: Would you tell us how positive karma works, because it could be postulated that when two people have satisfied all obligations, and have interacted in a positive way, that there would be no further need for them to meet in future lifetimes. They would move on to new experiences in new environments. Why do entities return again and again together on this plane?

---

[7] Also see chapter on Consciousness.

A: The number of times souls were reincarnated karmically depends on their evolution and what they have learned. Of course, the most important experience would be a relationship that has culminated in love and understanding. The amount of conscious ego would have to be completely dissolved before respect and understanding can be prevalent between two souls. In order to achieve this goal they must incarnate many, many times. For what you might perceive at your level of life as a completion of karma, is not necessarily so. When you enter the soul state you will realize what further experiences you must have with this other person: specifically, experiences where much emotion is emitted, either love or opposite, but mind you, these lifetimes are many.

Q: Are all lifetimes equally important?

A: Every lifetime is important. One no less than another. No matter how crippled, how poor, how degraded you may view an individual at a given time, it does not make that lifetime any less important than that one who has achieved a degree of balance. Whatever a soul is experiencing at that point is necessary, and he or she has brought upon themselves this form of existence.

On Soulmates, Counterparts and Life in Other Galaxies

Q: Can one individual soul experience life in different forms?

A: Yes, other forms of life with a similar vibratory rate to yours on Earth do exist. These life forms do not necessarily have to occur in human body. They may exist in different galaxies. At one time or another, all of you have experienced such forms of life.

Q: If a single soul is composed of different aspects, could not these aspects separate and inhabit different bodies on this plane at the same time?

A: Yes, as we have said before, if you would look upon yourself this evening you would see a part of the whole. The encompassing wholeness, the complete soul, once spiritual evolution on this planet has taken place, comes to be by the joining of its dissected parts. Each such part being an individual entity in itself which also goes forth to learn and grow. One part of soul, with its own individual personality, can reach a level of spiritual evolution far exceeding that which its counterpart is able to reach. One might be a very spiritual being while the other might be embedded in the worldly sphere. The evolved part might then leave and continue its evolutionary process in other spheres of learning. In time, through communicating with each other while in transitory state, and during times of stillness, each soul learns where the other resides, and the God force within one can speak to the God force in the other.

Only when all soul parts have mastered their difficult tasks can the soul complete its mission on this planet, and go on to other levels of learning. Let us just say: totally different ways of life and rates of growth may be experienced by counterparts of the same soul, yet ultimately the soul will be united.

Q: Are there ways to recognize counterparts of one's soul? Surely it must be easy to be misled by emotion. Is there a certain technique?

A: As an individual achieves a certain level of consciousness development, it becomes possible that a counterpart be brought into its life pattern on this plane. Recognition would take place, though, yet on a spirit and soul level. It would be a subconscious contact with much love and understanding between the individuals involved.

Q: Would you distinguish, please, between the counterpart of one's soul, and a soulmate?

A: Certainly. Soulmates are not parts of one's own soul. Souls who have traveled through many, many periods of time have gone through similar circumstances in the life experience and have become very, very close are soulmates. I must add, that once the evolution in this lifetime on Earth has attained this level of understanding, then these souls would separate and go different ways to experience whatever is still necessary for them in this universe.

Q: So, you say that parts of the same soul will join together one day after they have worked out all their karma—how long will this take?

A: Countless lifetimes are necessary for this, and much depends upon the swiftness of spiritual evolution within each part of the soul before it can be unified. At one time, there might be twelve parts of your soul all experiencing living, learning. Ultimately these forms of your soul are brought together in total balance.[8]

Q: What is the ultimate destiny of all souls?

A: This universe is without stagnation. Therefore, soul progresses, grows, learns the spiritual lessons, is able to clearly and lovingly understand what it is about, has harmonized mind, soul, and all organs within the body; in other words, has achieved true balance on this plane. Then that soul will no longer be returning to earth plane, for all lessons will have been learned. Soul is now free to begin new experiences at different levels of understanding. I might add, that these levels, of course, would be higher, more complicated, more spiritual, more

---

[8] In Theosophic literature there is an esoteric teaching concerning the seven inter-penetrating globes of our present "earth chain." Every soul that is incarnated is focused for now on this globe of the chain which we think of as Earth, while the more subtle and more gross aspects of the soul are experiencing on the other (more subtle or more gross) globes of earth. This is one way of saying that we never really leave the earth's force-field during this cycle of human evolution, but sense that we experience life on other planets. Theosophic teachings hold that the soul group presently on Earth must evolve through eons of time here before it will be correct for the evolution to leave Earth and begin on the next planet in our solar system.

demanding. But we are given only what we can handle at one time. We are never overburdened with responsibility. There are many new lessons and experiences to encounter once soul has left this Earth plane for good.

On Identical Twins, Soul Migration, Coma States, Schizophrenia, and the Possibility of a Body without Soul

Q: Are identical twins part of the same soul?

A: No, they are not, though it would seem likely. But the souls would not be brought together as one. These souls we speak of come into lifetime as twins from other souls who have been together many, many, many times. One would wish to call them soul-mates, for this would be as close as one could become without being of one soul, not always in harmony, or course, but always with much understanding of one another and knowing intuitively the needs and desires of the other without having to utilize speech patterns.

Q: Is it possible for a soul to transit into a different body mid-life, without leaving the Earth life; in other words, can I suddenly find myself with a different soul, or in a different body?

A: Quite impossible. The soul could not possibly take the place in another body unless transition has been culminated. In other words, death would have to occur before the soul could leave and take place in another body.

Q: Could there be a body without its own soul, filled with many fractions of different souls?

A: No, this would be impossible.

Q: What about schizophrenic beings?

A: Here we are not speaking of different souls. The soul is the unified life within the body. In mental diseases such as schizophrenia, we are dealing with possession. Outside negative entities take over the nervous system of a body and use it at will. Of course, this is not always the case, for indeed, there are different parts of the mind that sometimes are opened to hallucinatory imagination, but for the most part, in these types, we are speaking of possession.

Q: And what about a person who does not seem to have a soul at all, who is like a robot or seems to be dormant?

A: All living human beings have a soul. To be alive is to possess a soul. Once soul leaves body, transition would occur. Now then, individuals that you speak of, who seem dormant, who do not generate any energies, but seem to vegetate, these are beings who have succumbed to their own consciousness. They have not properly used their own will to aggressively defeat the problems presented to them. But these unresolved problems will most certainly present themselves again and again throughout their lifetimes until these lessons are learned and until these problems are rectified.

Q: Does such a soul decide this before being born, that it would have a lifetime of just being dormant and, perhaps, resting?

A: We can take that word "dormant" and use it in negative as well as positive manner. If you are speaking of a soul who comes into lifetime out of necessity to learn painful experiences brought on by previous karma and chooses not to face them but withdraws, then, of course, we are taking the word in negative context. But on the other extreme, we can use the word "dormant" in a positive way. You would recognize the difference quite easily. For one would show the negative qualities whereas the other would have more positive qualities and would, indeed, seem to be resting. But rather than word "resting," we would use word "observing" life, flowing with life, not adding much, but learning quietly. This is not negative.

Q: I was thinking, for instance, of a retarded person who lives in the maturity of a 5 year old all his or her life.

A: In this circumstance, what may be encountered is a soul not quite at ease with the sexual gender of its body, who has desired to come into such lifetime merely to observe, to learn how to use body. The life span of such individuals would often be short. It is only necessary for this type to learn and observe within the body. There is nothing more needed.

Q: How can a soul in a very damaged body which does not have measurable brain function learn at all? What of prolonged coma states?

A: The conscious mind would be, of course, dormant but the soul always learns from experience. It does not need the conscious mind to learn from these experiences.

On Marriage, Love, and Sex

Q: Is the institution of marriage a necessary one?

A: At this time, it is most necessary for mankind has not evolved to the point where it is unnecessary. This will come at one time. But believe me, we are far, far away from that time. It would be best to dismiss any thought that mankind has arrived at a point that marriage as an institution is unnecessary.

Q: What of destiny or karma in the choice of a marriage partner, or is such a choice a matter of free will?

A: Two questions again. Let us begin by saying that the will, or willfulness, dominates at times. Often this supersedes the pattern to which people should direct themselves. We can say here that, for the most part, most marriages are entered because of life patterns past and present.

Q: What is the purpose of marriage?

A: In as much as each and every one of you comes as an individual with needs and expressions all your own, the purpose is to learn from one another. It is opportunity to learn balance. The male learns subtlety, the female learns to be more assertive. Together, they create a third energy—the relationship. It, too, has needs. It must be nurtured and checked for signs of wear. It is into this energy that new souls may be drawn to experience life as your children. If two people seek to enter into the institution of marriage, it is well and good.

Q: Can you explain in more detail why we are sometimes incarnated as men, and sometimes as women?

A: Each sex brings with it its own sensitivities and its own traits. With the female part of the soul we have the part that is gentle, trusting, and, not always but usually, more sensitive. The psychic part of the soul would bear fruit much sooner within the female part of soul than with male. The male brings with it the necessary strength, aggressiveness, and when I speak of those things, I speak in positive manner, not negative.

So then, with male comes strength, aggressiveness, in most instances, practicality, which, of course, is most necessary in this life, for not every lifetime brings with it spiritual experiences where the soul walks the spiritual path, seeking, learning and growing.

There is much to be learned to balance this lifetime in the physical world and also the mental world. Thus, these qualities of the male counterpart are greatly needed and soul must learn from the mental and physical experiences. As you evolve, you find that these male and female traits will begin to merge together into one, so that eventually all would be into one and it would be complete. This, then, would be the complete balance of the three natures of mankind—mental, physical, and spiritual. One would look to your master Jesus as example of combining and balancing these natures.

Q: You said previously that in order to put sex on a more spiritual level, one should apply spiritual practices. Can you be more specific about this?

A: It is not necessary for the conscious mind to be totally subjected to physical desires. What transpires sexually between two individuals as they evolve spiritually is, of course, the obvious physical element. But the feelings, the emotions, the gratifications begin to enlarge, begin to broaden. Desire for physical fulfillment lessons by no means. However, desire for total concentration in this area begins to recede. The two individuals begin to understand that communion between the bodies is also communion between the souls. They will see that the union which takes place physically and spiritually is a beautiful thing indeed.

Q: According to Tantra Yoga, love and sex can be elevated to a superconscious level. What are your views on this?

A: That is what we speak of. To clarify this, let us continue: in order to achieve the communion of which we speak, both individuals must possess an understanding of what is transpiring here. Taking this premise, we would say that the fulfillment which the sexual act brings can be brought to a level where the two lovers begin to understand that the sexual act is only a part of the communion which each soul wishes to give to the other. It is in this giving to each other that one perceives that the physical union is just the beginning. The two individuals who have brought their energies and imparted these energies from one to the other, giving communion from one to the other, begin to understand the beauty of the sexual act, with the beauty of spiritual communion at this point.

Q: And this relationship then will also continue on the soul level?

A: This type of spiritual communication is indeed what transpires at the soul level. But this is what we are seeking always. For it is not necessary to communicate physically. What is necessary is that the spiritual communion between two people take place, that the love for each other take place.

Q: Is there a definite way of lovemaking on the soul level, if you were so inclined during your life on Earth? Is there a union between two beings as there is here?

A: The love of which you speak is transmitted in entirely different energy from that which you experience through your body there. To make it as simple as possible, it would be as if you and your loved one would not speak, would not touch, but through the powers of telepathic communication would express your love for each other and would be understood at that level.

Q: What do you think of group marriage, is it a healthy trend?

A: These are diversions. They will not last. Healthy or not is immaterial. If souls feel at this point that in their own consciousness the experience was good for them, then it may have been good. But over all, it would not last.

Q: Does love, ideal married love, serve to remove previous entanglements and to free the energies so that they may move toward evolution?

A: Toward awareness. Fear, fear of failure, fear of loss and the resulting miseries—possessiveness, jealousy, dishonesty—are all related to the ego. When love is learned and practiced, the self will begin to free itself from ego, from selfishness. When happiness no longer depends on conditions, it becomes a constant indweller of the self. This self then is free to become aware. Awareness is a necessary condition for the evolution of the soul.

Q: What are your views of "swinging," can it be of beneficial value at all?

A: These questions are immaterial. They do not concern spiritual growth. We are speaking in terms of ego satisfaction, not spiritual growth. It is not necessary to delve into these psychological and egotistical matters.

Q: Is divorce ever justified? Is it better for two people to separate if the staying together causes unbearable pain?

A: Why one soul, one individual now, would choose to stay with another depends, of course, entirely on their own consciousness, their own feelings of confidence and security within themselves. What they think of themselves, what they are getting from that relationship, what they are learning.

If the relationship is without pain and one can see continuous growth, then obviously this would be good. But there is no reason for two individuals to stay with each other when pain is involved. This is not the spiritual way; rather than growing, one retards the spiritual growth and one begins to assume upon itself karmic experiences in future with that soul. There is never any need for illogical pain regarding two individuals.

Q: Thank you.

On Consciousness

Q: We discussed in former sessions, "consciousness." You told us that consciousness does not depend on brain tissue. Does it depend on soul?

A: Indeed, for without soul or without the life-giving force there would be no consciousness. The brain is not able to produce consciousness without the assistance of the soul.

Q: Is the soul the same as consciousness?

A: Soul provides the consciousness. Let us define it in this way: One can say that without soul there is no consciousness. Without consciousness there can be a soul, for we are speaking in terms of limitations that an individual would bring about itself. Physically, one does not need to have thoughts, but soul can still inhabit body. When soul chooses to leave the physical body, there is no consciousness whatsoever. There are many aspects to soul. It is that part that God has chosen to present Himself as ourselves. We as He, He as us. Without his loving energies infusing us with this life, this soul, we would not exist. Soul then, has many aspects, one being consciousness.

Q: When does the soul enter the body?

A: The soul hovers around body during entire pregnancy. Life is taken with first breath of child.

Q: I do not quite understand. Does the soul enter the body at the time the sperm reaches the ovum, or is it at the time of birth?

A: Time of birth. Soul is lending energy to fetus during these months.

Q: Does the fetus have its own consciousness while residing in the mother's womb?

A: The fetus, at this stage, is a total physical organism that is relying for its life on the mother, of course. But the soul who shall be inhabiting that body is also around that area, that is, near the womb. The closer the fetus comes to being born, the closer the soul comes to the womb. In other words, for the sake of simplicity, let us say that at the beginning of pregnancy, the soul would be quite a distance away, but already would have begun the initial contact with the fetus, preparing itself for entering the body of the fetus. As the fetus grows older the soul then comes closer to the womb and so it goes until the final moment of birth, at which time the soul enters into the fetus before the child is pulled from the mother's womb.

Q: Thank you. I would still like to clarify this a little by asking you what kind of consciousness the fetus has while it is still within the mother?

A: The consciousness you are speaking of is totally at the physical level. We do not consider complete consciousness until the soul has entered the physical body, and the soul does this at the point when the fetus is becoming stronger and larger. The soul then begins to implement its own energies into the fetus, preparing itself for the entry. But the soul would have begun entry in partial basis, long before the birth occurs. But total, total entry is only accomplished just before the child is released from the womb.

Q: Does everything have consciousness, even matter, like a rock or a nail?

A: We are speaking, of course, in terms of relating to these consciousnesses, but for sake of simplicity, yes, to a degree, for everything is living. Everything you see and touch is alive within its own structure.

Q: Does it think, does a rock think?

A: Not in our terms, of course not, but it has within itself the idea of what it perceives itself to be, which is a rock. Limited consciousness, of course, but nonetheless, consciousness. For everything the Father, God, created has consciousness.

Q: When we die, are we ever without consciousness?

A: Consciousness permeates our life. Whether it be life in the physical form, or life living in this etheric form. Consciousness is always. One does not ever forget. Eventually, the human race will evolve to that point of spiritual capacity of finally utilizing all that the Father has given the human to enjoy, and to expand with. At that point in time, one will remember past lifetimes as clearly as one remembers yesterday.

Q: When you died in your last incarnation, Yan Su Lu, was there ever a time when you lost consciousness while making the transition?

A: There was a brief time when I had closed my eyes and knew that when I awoke again I would be out of my body. So, for one brief time, consciousness closed. I was not aware of the transition, but it would be, in your terminology, split second.

Q: So it was a very short time?

A: Indeed.

Q: And was the consciousness you woke up with again the same consciousness you had while you were alive?

A: To a degree, yes. But you must understand that the difference between that sort of lifetime and one of normal lifetime is very different. For the conscious mind that the average individual leaves at the time of transition does stay with it for quite some time until it is made to understand that it is no longer necessary to hold on to those thoughts and emotions that it had while in the body. And over a period of time, these thoughts and these emotions begin to fade away, and one does eventually lose contact with those thoughts.

Q: In one of our earlier sessions you stated that after transition the consciousness of an individual is exactly the same as before the transition. Does this mean that senile people with deteriorated personalities and intellect keep this senile consciousness after making the transition to the other side?

A: Quite the opposite. The senility involved at that time is purely physical. At transition, the consciousness is once again opened so that the soul consciousness is allowed to come through and oversee the decaying body left behind. What we were speaking of before was involving individuals who had consciousness at time of transition and were not involved in senility. But no, this is purely for the physical body. Consciousness does reawaken at this moment.

Q: Can you clarify for us once more the difference between earth-consciousness and soul-consciousness?

A: The earth-consciousness brings with it blockage of previous incarnations, previous lifetimes, specifically for purpose of intensified learning—the individual's lesson for this specific lifetime.

As we evolve, the earth-consciousness lessons and the spiritual soul-consciousness begins to take over. Therefore, glimpses of past incarnations, relationships, ideas, become much more cognizant to the individual, become much more meaningful, thereby that individual is able to draw upon specific past incarnations that deal with the present lifetime. But in order to achieve this openness of soul-consciousness, the individual must have taken and put himself or herself upon the spiritual path, and evolved to such a level that this consciousness does awaken, and/or open.

On Past Life Memories

Q: Why do some people seem to have easier access to past life memories than others?

A: We are speaking here in terms of spiritual evolution. As the souls progress upon the spiritual path, the unconsciousness awakens more easily to thoughts concerning past lifetimes. Memories will become much more important in that sort of lifetime.

The intuitiveness of the individual will focus upon the past lifetimes that deal with the specific problems in present lifetime. But these awakenings occur only when soul has put himself upon spiritual path and willingly accepts and desires to expand his or her knowledge in that realm.

Q: Are these past life memories ingrained in the person's brain tissue?

A: We are speaking of the soul in regard to a memory of past lifetime. It does not reside within the physical being of the individual, but within the spiritual centers, the spiritual power glands within the body. In particular the pineal gland and the solar plexus. These have much to do in aiding the opening of the consciousness.[9] But the opening occurs within the soul. The physical part acts as a catalyst to relate these experiences to the memories residing within the soul consciousness.

Q: So, in other words, you say that a person utilizes the psychic centers to widen his consciousness and to permit the admission of past incarnation memory?

A: Indeed.

Q: Not through the brain?

A: Indeed.

Q: In former sessions you have said that we learn about our inner reality in sleep state, not so much in dreams. How can our brain translate this learning which is transmitted telepathically, as you taught us, into knowledge and understanding?

A: Again, we must put aside the notion of the brain as being the only, the total communicator in these matters. When we are speaking of learning reality, spiritual reality, self-reality for that matter, in order for us to grow, we are speaking in terms of utilizing the spiritual centers within our bodies.

So, these realities which come to us during the sleep state will bypass the brain and, through the spiritual centers, make

---

[9] Yan Su Lu refers to the chakras. This reminded me of conversations I had many years ago with my late teacher Dr. Gustav Schmaltz about consciousness and chakras. It was his opinion that the chakra teachings of Indian Tantric Yoga contain physiological knowledge which will be important for the future of medical research in regard to the different levels of consciousness. See also: Gustav Schmaltz: *Komplexe Psychologie und Körperliches Symptom* (Stuttgart, Hippocrates Verlag, 1955), p. 115; Hiroshi Motoyama, *Theories of the Chakras: Bridge to Higher Consciousness* (Wheaton, IL: Theosophical Publishing House, 1981); Ken Wilber, *The Atman Project* (Wheaton, IL: Quest, Theosophical Publishing House, 1980).

the impression upon the consciousness that resides within the physical brain. But the brain is not the catalyst here, rather, the spiritual psychic centers would be the catalyst.

Q: Thank you.

On Talents, Abilities, and Genius

Q: What about talents? Did we bring these talents we seem to be born with from other lifetimes? For example, let's take a genius like Mozart, who was a great musician when he was only 5 years old. Would you say that such virtuosity had to do with former lives where he had acquired much knowledge about music?

A: Of course, yes. Regarding this matter, most definitely, yes. We have here a soul who has spent many lifetimes perfecting the ability within the musical realm. This is but one realm, one facet of the creativity that exists within the soul. Here we have what one would call genius. However, this is not genius at all, but simply one who has perfected his learning, his schooling in that field.

The talent for creativity is a spiritual quality. It is within the power of the soul to expand its own creativity, its own creative talents. If the soul chooses to expand its knowledge in one or more of these realms during its many lifetimes, it does so. We all at one time become perfected in a chosen realm. These creative talents I speak of are perfected not only on this planet, but on other planets with similar vibrations. The need for perfecting these areas of creativity persists.

So, if a soul does not perfect all her creative talents here, she, indeed, will in other areas, other life spheres, other forms of living beyond this planet.

On Guardian Angels

Q: What is a "guardian angel," do they exist?

A: We would rather not use the title of "guardian angel," for as we discussed before, each individual in the incarnate state has many teachers. These teachers come to the individual for varying reasons. One would be for spiritual reasons, another for health, and another for, let us say, not exactly materialistic reasons, but to provide the individuals with the guidance to avail themselves the opportunity according to the pattern of their lifetime. But bear in mind each one of these teachers has, in his own right, evolved to the level of spiritual being.

In other words, the teachers have learned much more than the individual they are with. It is true that these are guardians, but they do not interfere as that word might imply. To do so would usurp the free will of individual. They are there for guidance and also to assist, when called upon, be it through meditation, or through prayer. They are there for this specific purpose.

The word "angel" was a title given to these teachers many centuries ago by the Christians who decided to put more emphasis on the spirituality of these beings. But the terminology is not completely true in that sense. These teachers do not have so-called "wings" which enable them to fly, not at all. They are their own individual spirit and conceive themselves in whatever manner they desire, but it would be on the etheric level.

Q: Does everyone have a teacher like Charles has you, Yan Su Lu?

A: Indeed. Throughout this universe teachers are with all living things. You must understand that the Father in His universal consciousness has appointed to all living things those who would guide and direct. These are teachers. In your religious connotations you would speak of them as "angels." We are here for all of you, to guide you in your hour of need, in your hour of meditation, in your hour of prayer. We are the ones who are there to respond to you in all ways that we can without, of course, interfering with your own free will and your own karma.

On Dying

Elisabeth Kübler-Ross, the noted psychiatrist, has done pioneer work on death and dying. She explains the death experience to children as follows: "Death is simply a shedding of the physical body, like the butterfly coming out of a cocoon. And the only thing you lose is something you don't need anymore—your physical body."[10]

Thales, the Greek philosopher, taught that there was no true death, that dying makes no difference. From modern science in Bob Toben's book, *Space, Time & Beyond*, we have a statement that clarifies Thales' point of view: "There is no death, only a change of awareness, a change of cosmic addresses."[11]

It seems that people who have attained a higher consciousness regard dying as a transition to a new phase of development. The renowned spiritual teacher, Paramahansa Yogananda, described death as the transition of a soul from the physical to an astral body.[12]

In describing the death experience Sri Sathya Sai Baba has said: "Death is a state very much like sleep. The individual discards his body like an old worn out suit of clothes. Only the body perishes. As the mind has no physical form, it does not perish with the body, and thought activity persists even after the death of the body."[13]

In my practice, I have often experienced a healthy person turning away from discussing the subject of death. He or she would more readily discuss sex. It is a peculiar reversal that our society has experienced in the last hundred years; then, sex was a forbidden subject and death was acceptable. Now, death is forbidden and sex is shouted about. But both are inescapably with us, of course, and it does great harm to avoid looking at the inescapable, especially in the face of the tremendous fear the average person has of death.

---

[10] From a filmed interview with Kay Croissant and Kathy Dees for the 1978 Exhibit of Continuum in Los Angeles.

[11] Bob Toben, *Space, Time & Beyond* (New York, Bantam, 1983), p. 12.

[12] See *Man's Eternal Quest*, p. 273.

[13] Eruch B. Fanibunda, *Vision of the Divine* (Bombay, E.B. Fanibunda, n.d.), p. 105.

This was what I had in my mind when I asked Yan Su Lu the following:

Q: Can you explain the death experience to us?

A: The word "death" has much negative connotation in your society, and in fact, in your world at this time. Yet, it is only through death that the soul is released from its mission in this lifetime and proceeds to grow and learn again in another. It would be much more positive to think of death as a transition from the physical to the ethereal dimension.

Q: Is the death experience different for a young person and a person who has lived a long and full life?

A: The amount of years that one has in this lifetime has no bearing at all upon what the soul will respond to once it leaves the body. If a young person has indeed gained spiritual wisdom in the few years that he is on Earth, then his transition becomes one of simplicity, for he already knows what to expect once transition takes place, and would even eagerly await teachers and loved ones to assist him. The confusion lies in the souls, rather personalities, that have had no spiritual training during this lifetime, have had no desire for communication with the Father, and have clung to archaic beliefs pertaining to the certain religious philosophies that that personality may have adhered to at that time. With all the different religions of your world, each one preaching different ways to heaven, different ways to avoid hell, and what to expect after death, one would listen to this and become confused during transition. But we here already expect this and already anticipate what is best for the soul at that time.

Q: Would it be more difficult for someone who does not believe in God to make the transition, than someone who has definite beliefs in a structured heaven?

A: It would be much easier if the personality had had some form of belief in the hereafter, rather than the personality who was devoid of any spiritual inclination. This is the personality that so many times is not only confused but very fearful of the teachers that come to him after transition.

Q: When we die, do we die in stages, or suddenly all at once?

A: In matter of aging, the death state takes place in stages. Much preparation is taken. But, in so-called accidents, and I say "so-called," then of course the soul, even though it has brought itself to that point of departure from physical life, it still becomes rather traumatic to him or her. But soul who has no need for that traumatic type of departure is able to make transition in more peaceful manner.

Q: How can we overcome the fear of death?

A: By immersing oneself in the ideas and philosophy of rein- carnation. For by understanding that there is no death per se, but only transition period from one physical body to another, then we would understand that there is no need to fear the transition known as death.

Q: Where do the dead go? After leaving the body, does the soul always pass through what we call the "astral sphere?"

A: I would not wish to label it in that manner. Let us say that the soul leaving the body is quickly surrounded by teachers and made to feel as comfortable as possible. She is given the opportunity to either stay with the body for as long as she desires, or to continue on with teachers, knowing that much greater things are before her. It is her decision, and it is not rushed into. These things are taken quite seriously, and we understand that at point of transition many, many souls come to us frightened and in despair and very confused. And so all the time that they require is given to them. It is their decision.

Q: We asked you, in former sessions, where confused souls would reside after transition. You mentioned that they would undergo treatment in a place similar to our hospitals. Could you tell us more about this?

A: Indeed. Again, for the sake of clarity, or simplicity, let us call them "hospitals." The souls who are weary or confused do reside here for some time, depending upon the soul's acceptance of where it is and for that matter, where it has been. These hospitals have within them the teachers of that soul.

Many times if loved ones are evolved enough to the point that they understand the workings of the law, they will be placed alongside the confused soul to facilitate the awakening, and to ease the transition from confusion to reality. Alongside these loved ones will be the teachers of that soul who are always present.

In small quantities the soul will then begin to understand the surroundings, the necessity for its being there. The soul will be surrounded by love vibrations, for this hospital is one of love and understanding.

So, the soul may be confused for a while but sooner or later, succumbs to the tremendous amount of love that is given to it at this time. Once confusion has ceased, then the process of establishing itself in this area, establishing who it is, what it has been, are fundamental things that must take place. The soul must understand its past, and little by little it is able to recognize with the help of its teachers, the mistakes that were made in past lifetimes; not only mistakes but also the positive goals that were accomplished. The soul is always free to come and go as it wishes but once souls understand the reason for being there, they choose to stay for obvious reasons. For only through this initial contact with their teachers can they begin to understand themselves and what is necessary for their continued evolvement.

On Contact of a Departed Soul with a Loved One Left Behind

Q: Can a departed soul get in touch with a loved one left behind in order to convey a message or a warning, and how would that happen?

A: This would take place through the energy form of telepathy. Contact would occur in the sleep state, or it could happen in the conscious state, at which time the energies imparted by the soul in the ethereal world would then begin to direct the individual's thoughts with deep concentration. Here I might add, that it is not easy to communicate with those who are not aware of the existence of life after. It is with these individuals that much concentrated effort must be made in order to establish contact. But disregarding belief, contact can be made.

At one time, a small amount of this energy could seep into the conscious mind of the individual contacted, and thought could be seeded there. The best time to utilize this communication would be in the sleep state.

Q: Can a departed soul lend his or her energies to a loved one left behind, who is aware of continuing existence, and who is in need of guidance?

A: The departed entity can assist a loved one on this level. But if that soul wishes to progress itself and wishes to make use of the efforts undertaken on its behalf, mainly the revitalizing of soul consciousness so that soul understands what has transpired while it was on Earth, and what now must continue in the learning processes of the etheric world, it must go on.

If, however, that departed entity should choose not to proceed along these paths and wishes to remain earthbound in order to assist a loved one, that is its choice and its choice would be heeded.

The departed one would not take the place of teacher, for the individual has his or her own teachers. The loved one would be there for comfort rather than direction, for the teachers would know, much better than the departed one, what is best for the individual.

So, assistance would come through comfort and the loving energies and vibrations sent, and thought waves to the one left behind. As far as superseding or taking place of teacher, no, this could not happen.

Q: Would it be retarding for the soul in the etheric world if contact with a person left behind on earth remained for a long time? Is it better to let go?

A: It is always better to release the ties from either the dear departed, or from the living one. We must understand that it would enhance the evolutions of both souls if indeed the ties were broken. To release a loved one is, within human eyes, justifiably painful, and this would be painful to the departed one as well.

Now then, the departed soul would not retard its progress if it should remain for a short amount of time. Many souls do wish to stay for a while, to oversee their loved ones and to understand fully within themselves that all is well, that what has transpired was necessary and that the soul had chosen that time and place of transition to the etheric world. There is a short period of time that most souls do remain earthbound before they proceed with their own evolution on the etheric side.

Q: When on the soul level, while still fondly remembering our Earth days, are we at that stage, surrounded by the things we knew, like houses, plants and animals?

A: The consciousness of the departed soul remains exactly as it was before transition. The soul sees whatever it wishes to behold. It can perceive itself into a realm of whatever would be beauty to its eyes, spiritual eyes at this point. And, until this consciousness subsides, it will dwell at this level. It is a most peaceful level, we might add. Ultimately, as the soul beings to understand the lessons and directions that it must now begin to take, this consciousness will slowly recede, not regress, but recede and eventually will be forgotten. Earth consciousness does remain with the departed soul for some time. It is very peaceful and quite beautiful.[14]

Q: When we die, do we meet loved ones on the other side?

---

[14] See also the section on Consciousness.

A: Many times, when one leaves the physical body, there are relatives, let us say, that would be waiting, yes. Not always, but it does happen. This can only take place, of course, if these souls have not already prepared themselves for incarnation. And so, many times one will find friends of similar age there, rather than mother or father who might at that time be on their journey toward a new incarnation. Unless, of course, those souls have chosen not to incarnate. It is their choice and then they would be there to meet the loved ones.

On Suicide

Q: Is it ever justified to terminate one's own life? I am thinking of, for instance, the Buddhists who set fire to their bodies in an effort to protest unbearable conditions, and who, by sacrificing themselves, try to help others, which is actually an act of love . . .

A: An act of love, but a misused act of love. There is no need for this action. While it may help the conscious mind to feel that it has dramatically shown the world its convictions and hopefully, by this deed, would change the attitudes, we might add that these things do not assist.

While this is not the type of suicide most people indulge it, and that would be the complete negation and misuse of its own free will, this individual you have cited would not experience the same difficulties in perceiving what is here, once it comes to this place. But it would have to learn that one does not end karma in this way. It must learn that it must proceed with its mission; for the pain that comes with life is always justified for this individual. These pains are but opportunities, lessons, and they must be learned and they must be accomplished.

Q: Now I'm speaking of a person who commits suicide for the usual reasons, like not being able to face reality, failure, and so on. Does such a soul, by this act, distance itself from its teachers, guides, the divine, and get lost and confused? Must it wander in confusion before it once again finds itself where it was before?

A: There is never a disconnection on the part of the teacher. If an individual brings itself to the point where it cannot face the realities of life and commits the act of suicide, it will usually enter the etheric world with great fear and mistrust of all and anything it perceives.

The teacher is always there to assist the soul. It is the soul that chooses to disconnect from the teacher. But it never does so completely. Souls who enter this realm with such fear consciousness and mistrust will attract many like souls. This soul will be earthbound for a long time. It will communicate only with those of its own kind. It will live in a very lonely and fearful world which it conjures up itself.

The teacher is always there, talking, listening, and assisting in any way that it can to help this soul understand where it is, what it is, and what it must become.

Gradually, these souls do understand, listen, and communicate with their teachers. At this point they are able to receive proper assistance from teachers. The teachers are always in contact with the individual. Always!

Q: Does it take a long time until a soul such as this can reincarnate again into physical body?

A: Oh yes. Speaking of this small minority, compared to the thousands upon thousands of souls who come to this realm, these who wantonly give up their lives are a small minority. Within this group no one can foretell how much time an individual soul will take before it understands and communicates with its teacher.

On Hellish Realms, Murderers, Failure

Q: Does hell exist?

A: In the sense that it implies a most negative state of being, yes. In both planes of living, etheric and incarnate, exists this so-called "hell." In the incarnate state, mankind, through its own negative consciousness, brings upon itself such problems that it indeed would seem as though it would be hell. But these are man-made and only there because mankind foolishly avoids the availability of spiritual guidance and insists upon living a most negative life. In this sense people create their own hell.

The discarnate state is a realm where souls who have lived a life of complete degradation and violence, disregarding all moral laws, have chosen not to avail themselves of the guidance that their own teachers offer them. They set about to find equal souls, in other words, like themselves. This is quite easily done because over centuries of time many souls have gathered together, compounding the problems that existed in physical state and now exist in the etheric state. These souls live in a realm which could be best described as the antithesis of what has been described as "hell," for in this realm there is no heat. There is no fire. Rather, they live and exist in tremendous amount of coldness and dampness.

They suffer unnecessarily, but their own consciousness has been so embedded in negativity that they cannot see themselves beyond the state to which they have brought themselves. They have attached themselves to this realm foolishly, for they find negative comfort with souls that act and think as they. It is quite tragic and it saddens us to see this, but fortunately, one soul after the other, in due time, accepts the assistance of their teachers and brothers who are always there waiting for them, speaking to them, asking them to come with them.

Q: Could you tell us what happened to the soul of Adolph Hitler?[15]

A: This entity has not been incarnated at this point. The soul lives in a state that he has willingly put himself into. A state of confusion, and sorrow that is a tremendous amount of distorted energies. These energies are within a realm of his choosing which is most unpleasant.

---

[15] Normally, Yan Su Lu did not speak of personal situations, but his answer to this question was immediate.

When I say that it is unpleasant, I am not really able to tell you the degree of unpleasantness that exists. It is unfortunate that these souls bring themselves to this point, but the ego involved is so immense that they are not able to recognize the degree of the mistakes. Once they recognize the need for assistance, their degree of experiences, their karma, will be so physically great, and of course, they know this and most choose to withhold a decision for a long time, for they would, out of necessity, come back to Earth in a very limited physical capability. The soul would experience great abuse, debaucheries, upon itself. Not once, but through many lifetimes. And so, the decision to begin this path of undoing which one has created is most difficult, but still most necessary, and eventually will transpire.

As I have said before, this type of soul is so embedded in negativity, sometimes it takes, in your terminology, centuries before they are able to release themselves from this realm.

Q: Does this mean that someone like Hitler will have to suffer murder being inflicted upon himself over six million times?

A: No. He will experience the physical feeling of the unpleasantness that he inflicted on others, but not six million times, no.

Q: Is it possible that he could be incarnated as an animal instead of a human being?

A: This is impossible. For the human consciousness only incarnates within the human body.

Q: Do all who commit violent crimes and murder end up in this realm?

A: The souls that exist in this realm have—through more than one incarnation—utilized their negative powers to a great degree. And it is only at this time that they then bring themselves to this realm. But it would take more than one incarnation involving one killing, let us say. That soul who would bring about the negative transition (murder) of another would not be too anxious to continue upon this path in this realm. For he would understand the misgivings of his act and he could remain earthbound for some time in a state of fear and confusion, but not to the degree of the negative confusion that exists with the soul of Adolph Hitler.

Q: Is there such a thing as failure, or is it all simply learning?

A: Failure is a word that people have brought into vocabulary to excuse themselves from the necessary directions that they should have taken. Failure is a negative word in spirit. Lessons are positive. We do not recognize the terminology "failure."

On Choosing a New Incarnation

Q: Is the self made up of the sum of previous life patterns? In other words, are former incarnation experiences a part of the present self?

A: Within each incarnation the soul brings with it the experiences from previous lifetimes. But in as much as there are so many lessons to be learned with an unevolved soul, one must take these lessons sometimes, one by one. In other words, the soul will choose before he enters his incarnate state, the situation that will best enable him or her to learn from one or more specific problems that have occurred in the past.

For souls, unfortunately, do not always learn lessons in one lifetime. They choose to disregard opportunities and experiences that are given to them to achieve this pattern, this goal, to overcome problem. Many lifetimes may be involved before this can be accomplished. Therefore, let us state most certainly that very few souls are able to overcome their past problems in one lifetime. So, in such a case, the soul will continue to bring about these circumstances which quite possibly existed in past incarnations. He will bring these about in present life and if that is not learned, he will come again until such lesson has been learned.

Q: How does a reincarnating personality know which parents it wants to choose, or which womb it wants to inhabit as a fetus?

A: Long before the act of incarnation takes place, the soul has, with the help of brothers and teachers, the soul has been schooled, let us say, in the areas of what it needs most to learn in the coming incarnation. The soul decides by itself.

No one tells the soul that it must incarnate, that it must pick certain parents. The soul does this willingly, voluntarily. But it has, at its disposal, the wisdom of its teachers to draw upon. The teachers present the ideal parents, environment, race, etc., concerning the coming lifetime. The soul is aware of whatever pain may exist in that lifetime, for in all problems that must be overcome there is a certain amount of pain that comes with this. The soul accepts the situation, knowing that this is the way for it to overcome the problem which has existed in the past, and therefore freely chooses to proceed with that pattern. These patterns concerning parents, friends, loved ones, are all brought before him and he knows what to expect and goes then willingly.

Q: How does the attraction between parent and the new soul take place? What sort of force draws these souls together?

A: Each incarnating soul brings with it a pattern for that lifetime. If two souls, male and female, meet and decide to have a child, it is not by accident. Before these two souls came into this lifetime it had been decided that they would meet, given the situation, and fulfill the pattern. They would have a child. The soul who is preparing for incarnation understands that pattern, views it, sees it, accepts his own, and also the parents pattern for, of course, he will be part of that environment. So, in every case, it is patterns we speak of, patterns that each soul has willingly accepted.

Time Span between Lives, How Many Lives, Soul Evolution, Solar Systems, Understanding God and Our Purpose

Q: Would there be a minimum of time for a soul to understand what it needs to learn and then to make the decision to come back?

A: There is no set time. Let us say that average time span in between incarnation is anywhere between thirty and one hundred of your years.

Q: It has been said that we can be reincarnated millions of times. Is that so?

A: I would not use the term "millions." While this is true, indeed, it is not true for this planet. Millions of times reincarnating in other forms of expression, yes, but for the purpose of this planet, let us say thousands.

Q: When you speak of forms of expression, do you mean other forms of expression on other planets?

A: Indeed.

Q: Can you elaborate on these planets, are there many planes on which you can reincarnate?

A: There are all forms of existence. Not necessarily as you experience your physical, mental and spiritual. But there are forms of physical expressions.

Q: Can you describe for us what the other side looks like?

A: It is understood what you mean. Mental forms exist in other parts of solar system for specific purpose of evolution. It is only one other form of expression the infinite Father has allowed to happen.[16] And in this way, these expressions within their own vibratory growth, learn and grow and venture out to other forms of expression. Each and every planet has its own form of expression. This does not mean that while you reside on this planet you automatically would continue to experience other lives, other expressions, within your own solar system. This is not true. There are many other solar systems, some very similar in vibratory rate as your planet here. Thus, your souls can also go to other solar systems and experience other forms of life, and in most cases, these other parts of your soul do reside there, in forms of energy and expression that vibratorily are close to the condition you are experiencing here.

Q: Does a soul subsist on sun energy? What sustains a soul?

A: You must understand that the physical functions are set aside at this level of existence. Let us put the soul in a proper place and put the body beside it. You understand, of course, the physical functions that must transpire, but do not seem to understand that the soul has no need for these functions whatsoever. I am speaking of the necessity for food and drink. The partaking of these things does not exist here in any form, nor does it exist in thought. In other words, soul does not think nourishment.

The energy flow that comes to the soul and leaves the soul is everflowing and everliving. It is a manner of energy that one does not think of. It is there. You do not think of the air you breathe, so soul has no thought concerning breath or nourishment once it enters this etheric world. It is there.

Q: Why, in the first place, do we exist? Or why do we have to be born? Why couldn't we stay from the beginning with the divine principle, what separated us?

---

[16] See Paramahansa Yogananda's *Autobiography of a Yogi*, chapter on The Resurrection of Sri Yukteswar. Self-Realization Fellowship, 1946.

A: Your own consciousness separated you from the beginning. For at one time all souls were what you would call "masters" on this planet. It was through evolution that these souls in totality allowed themselves to believe that they were greater than the Father. And this is what your religion would call the fall of mankind. It was the conscious man, the ego, taking dominance over the spiritual and as this became a way of life at that point, the spiritual aspect could no longer take presence, the conscious began to take dominance and continued over many, many, many evolutions.

What happened became a great chasm between spiritual mind and physical ego conscious mind. And spiritual was left behind. With this, as each soul reincarnated, the conscious became so dominant that at one point in your evolutions the spiritual was but a small seed next to huge tree of all conscious mind.

Q: When we reach the final stages of what I would call liberation, we would say we are one with the Divine. Is there a better explanation you could give to us?

A: The sole purpose of your existence on this planet is to have in balance the three aspects of mankind. That is, as you know, the spiritual, mental, and physical. When a soul has evolved on this planet to the point where he has domination over these three areas and has mastered them, then it is no longer necessary for that soul to incarnate again on this planet. We are speaking of teachers. Reaching this point takes many incarnations on spiritual path. But it is within each and every one of you to attain the same goals as the other great teachers. For you all possess the same power and that is found within you.

Q: Is it possible for us to understand God? Is there any way to describe this so that we are able to know what that actually means—God?

A: This is a question that can only be answered by yourself. For each conscious mind interprets the infinite Father in his or her own way, and only by seeking and asking for these answers can you, on a personal level, understand them yourself.[17]

Q: What is the best way to apply all of the knowledge you have given us in our daily lives?

A: There is so much to say, and we could go on for hours and hours. Let us say, in order for your own growth to allow itself to develop in most positive spiritual way, all that you would look at, all that you would speak to, would be with love.

For from love comes understanding, tolerance, sensitivities. The wanting to help, the desire to do all that you can for your fellow humans, without asking anything in return. For when we begin to applaud ourselves for our good deeds, then in essence, those deeds are not good, for if one wishes recognition for the positive things we do in our life, then we are speaking of ego, and ego is and shall always be the downfall of mankind. For the Father in His wisdom in giving us and allowing us free will, knew that in giving this to us, evil would rear its ugly head; but this is necessary to learn difference between good and bad.

And, as we cleanse ourselves of this ego, and move toward that spiritual path and become that which our Father has ordained us to be, then the world love takes on much greater significance upon our life. For then one sees all things through the eyes and consciousness of love, and the necessity to argue, to criticize, to fight, to war, then dissolves. For these things have no place when love abounds.

There was a long silence. I looked at Yan Su Lu. His hands, always folded during his trance states, sank slowly into his lap, and his face changed back to that of Charles Roberts again. Inwardly, I smiled. I felt with this message of unconditional love we had come to the end of our journey together.

---

[17] Here I would like to quote C.G. Jung (Time Magazine, 14, II, 1955): "I would not say, I believe, I know. I had the experience of being gripped by something that is stronger than myself, something that people call God."

Conclusion

In my end is my beginning—
(last words of Mary Queen of Scots)

And so, who is Yan Su Lu? Is he that most spiritual part of Charles Roberts' total consciousness, the two-million-year-old wise one that Jung believed to be a part of everyone? Or is Yan Su Lu a separate entity? Or the guardian angel of our childhood hopes? I know one thing without doubt: Yan Su Lu was capable of moments of great wisdom. The fact that he presented himself as a guardian figure is a comforting promise for many who may never experience such a vivid externalization of our heritage of inner wisdom.

Is there really a wise man or mother within us who watches as we leave this life, ready to prepare us for another and even greater experience, who helps us to integrate and perfect our consciousness into the soul-level of our immortal self? I have come to believe that there is such a one. In the East this higher aspect is called Krishna or Buddha-consciousness; in the West it is called Christ-consciousness. We seek it all our lives, but most of us do not consciously know that we do. We have a difficult time recognizing the advice of our higher self, or even acknowledging its existence. Certainly the thing we commonly call our conscience has a connection with this better part of us, for it instinctively distinguishes between good and evil.

But, what if we come to a point of awareness where we wish to contact this higher self more directly, establish a relationship with our own personal Yan Su Lu, for example? Is it just a matter of saying: "I invite my wise self to speak to me," and then sitting back, receptive to anything that floats onto the screen of our thoughts?

My advice would be: If you do hear a voice or see an image, challenge its validity, and pursue it to its source. Remember, a mind that is in a passive, non-discriminating state, or simply a state of curiosity, is subject to self-delusion. Somewhere inside us may be this wise one, and foolish ones as well, that respond to events around us. The human consciousness appears to exist on a number of levels at once, probably far more than we are able to understand with our limited consciousness.

If the voice you hear promises you wonderful things, and flatters you unconscionably, how truly wise must it be? Listen to its pronouncements. Are they universal and constructive? Do they seem to be for you alone, or for a better understanding of the universe? Which of your many selves have you reached out to contact?

One more advisory: Before you respond to this inner voice, be sure that your action will not harm anybody and is not for the gratification of your ego. The currents flowing from the depths of our subconscious can be dangerous if not carefully approached. My experiment with Charles and Yan Su Lu was hopefully done with an awareness of the constant pitfalls.

According to Jung, the wise being as a Personification of the Spiritual Principle is eternally present in each of us. It is simply a question of how our consciousness chooses to deal with it, how we are to bring it forth. I had opportunities to observe the subtle variations in the personality of Yan Su Lu. There were few times he would hesitate and his words would lose their customary depth and focus. At times this faltering seemed almost a delaying tactic and I had to ask whether Charles in his trance state was shying back and forth trying to establish a clear connection with the source of his wisdom, Yan Su Lu.

When I questioned Yan Su Lu, he told me that sometimes he had to "rotate" an idea until he could make a proper link between Charles' mental state and his articulation. Whatever the case, once this contact was made, the link between Charles and his teacher became a firm one.

• • •

My original intention was to help Charles ease outbursts of rage which were causing deep unhappiness. After the Irish regression he began to show a change. It wasn't to be a cure-all, of course. Charles still had decisions to make, whether, for one, to divorce his wife Dorothy and remarry. But this time with Yan Su Lu seemed to offer an opportunity for re-evaluation in many ways. He remarried and divorced and is now married to Dorothy again, quite happily, and has a far more satisfying and responsible career in a position that requires a considerable degree of tact and wisdom.

Yan Su Lu has been, perhaps, more stimulating to me than to Charles, although I don't doubt that he is glad to be able to reach out to a spiritual source and to continue the process of self-realization which had been triggered by Yan Su Lu.

The world's greatest spiritual teachers advise us to look for the God within ourselves, and Yan Su Lu echoes that advice. The Indian philosopher and mystic, Paramahansa Yogananda, wrote: "The souls of all creatures, through unconscious recollection of their divine origin, tend naturally to seek their Source."

A spiritual evolution taking place in the universe must move toward a goal of ultimate unity with all life. We may waver in our focus, sometimes seeming to be wise, other times merely hoping we have the appearance of wisdom. Meanwhile, we will keep searching for the deeper elements of our being. We will study the words of the wise ones who have told us how to build a bridge joining us to our source.

Yan Su Lu is a focal point of the human search for wisdom. Even a glimpse of higher knowledge can be healing to both mind and body. The tensions we live with in our concept of being finite and mortal can be eased. We can become more secure and comfortable in a new infinite universe and dare to accept our own immortality.

Jung, a daring explorer of new dimensions said it well: "No one can say where man ends." And Emerson, the American philosopher and transcendentalist spoke of boundless man:

> As a plant upon the earth, so a man rests upon the bosom of God: he is nourished by unfailing fountains, and draws at his needs inexhaustible power. Who set the bounds to the possibility of man?

I once asked Yan Su Lu for his definition of the goal of mankind. He answered: "To have mastered this lifetime as Jesus had."

EPILOGUE
By E. Stanton Maxey, M.D.*

Having now read this work, you are aware that a central hub invokes reincarnation. One cannot escape remembering it was through hypnosis that Edgar Cayce stumbled into an awareness of reincarnation. Eugene Jussek, in publishing his research, has joined such notables as Ian Stevensen (*Twenty Cases Suggestive of Reincarnation*), Joan Grant and Denys Kelsey (*Many Lifetimes*), and Raymond A. Moody, Jr. (*Life After Life*). Like Ian Stevensen, Eugene Jussek has found old records which convince all but the most skeptical that, under deep hypnosis, some curiosity of the human mind yields memories of other life scenarios from other, often ancient, time frames.

But, ever the probing detective, Eugene Jussek stumbled over the idea that a spiritually superior father-type figure may in some way oversee each of our lives. Grasping the significance of this possibility, Dr. Jussek became relentless in his pursuit until the documented dialogue which you have in hand came forth.

Has Dr. Jussek been midwife to the birth of a spiritual reality which is new for our time? Or is this all nothing more than a figment of Charles Roberts' mind? Who can say?

What can be said is that the possibility elucidated by Dr. Jussek's research is a gauntlet thrown down before each one of us. We may (must?) delve deep within our own beings seeking out our own Yan Su Lu. Such a quest augurs well the meaningful uncovering of hitherto unknown spiritual elements within each one of us.

---

* Former Research Director of the John E. Fetzer Energy Medicine Research Institute, A.R.E. Clinic, Phoenix, AZ.

The quest assures discovery. Only a short reflection upon certain events and dreams of this lifetime forces me to understand that no few of us have, are, and will encounter hierarchical spiritual beings who seek to guide our steps and enlighten our paths.

BIBLIOGRAPHY

Benson, Herbert, M.D. *Beyond the Relaxation Response*. New York: Times Books, 1984.

Boeth, Jennifer. "God, Mind, and Free Will: The Scientific Evidence," in *Self-Realization Fellowship Magazine*, Vol. 55, No. 3, 1984.

Brown, Barbara. *New Mind, New Body*. New York: Bantam. 1974.

————. *Stress and the Art of Biofeedback*. New York: Bantam, 1977.

Brownwell, George B. *Reincarnation*. Santa Barbara, CA: The Aquarian Ministry, nd.

Brunton, Paul. *A Search in Secret India*. York Beach, ME: Samuel Weiser, 1970, 1984.

Croissant, Kay, and Dees, Catherine. *Continuum: The Immortality Principle*. San Bernadino, CA: Franklin Press, 1978 (Public exhibit and book).

David-Neel, Alexandra. *Magic and Mystery in Tibet*. New York: Claude Kendall, 1932.

Diels, H., ed. "Commentary on a Fragment of Heraclitus' Teachings," in *Doxographi Greaci*, 1879.

Eccles, John Carew, and Daniel N. Robinson. *The Wonder of Being Human: Our Brain, Our Mind*. New York: Free Press, division of MacMillan, 1984.

Faribunda, E. B. *Vision of the Divine*. Bombay: E. B. Faribunda, nd.

Goldman, Burt. *How to Better Your Life with Mind Control*. Tarzana, CA: Silva Publishing Co., 1980.

Green, E., Green, A., and D. Walters. "Voluntary Control of Internal States: Psychological and Physiological," in *Journal of Transpersonal Psychology*, 11: 1-26, 1970.

Gris, Henry, and William Dick. *The New Soviet Psychic Discoveries*. New York: Warner, 1978.

Grof, Stanislav. *The Adventure of Self-Discovery*. Albany: State University of New York Press, 1987.

Hoeller, Stephan A. *The Gnostic Jung and the Seven Sermons of the Dead*. Wheaton, IL: Theosophical Publishing House, 1982.

Jacobi, Jolande, ed., in collaboration with R. F. C. Hull. *C. G. Jung: Psychological Reflections: A New Anthology of his Writings*, Bollingen Series XXXI. Princeton, NJ: Princeton University Press, 1953, 1970.

Jacobson, E. *Progressive Relaxation*. Chicago: Chicago University Press, 1938.

Jeans, James. *The Mysterious Universe*. New York: E. P. Dutton, 1932.

Jung, C. G. *Memories, Dreams, Reflections*. Recorded and edited by Aniela Jaffé, translated by Richard and Clara Winston. New York: Pantheon, 1961.

Kelsey, Denys, and Joan Grant. *Many Lifetimes*. Garden City, NY: Doubleday, 1967.

Kroger, William S. *Clinical and Experimental Hypnosis*. Philadelphia: J. B. Lippincott, 1963.

Kroger, William S., and William D. Fezler. *Hypnosis and Behavior Modification: Imagery Conditioning*. Philadelphia: J. B. Lippincott, 1976.

Kübler-Ross, Elisabeth. *On Death and Dying*. New York: Macmillan, 1969.

Moody, Raymond A. *Life After Life*. Covington, GA: Mockingbird Books, 1975.

Motoyama, Hiroshi. *Theories of the Chakras: Bridge to Higher Consciousness*. Wheaton, IL: Theosophical Publishing House, 1981.

Ornstein, Robert. *The Psychology of Consciousness*. London: Penguin Books, 1972.

Osborne, Arthur. *Ramana Maharshi and the Path of Self-Knowledge*. York Beach, ME: Samuel Weiser, 1973.

Osis, Karlis, and Erlander Haraldson. *At the Hour of Death*. New York: Avon, 1977.

Prabhu, R. K. *Mohan-Mala: A Gandhi Rosary*. Ammedabad, India: Navajivan Publishing House, 1949.

Puharich, Andrija. *Beyond Telepathy*. Garden City, NY: Doubleday, 1962.

Ring, Kenneth. *Heading Toward Omega*. New York: Quill, Morrow, 1984.

Ritchie, George. *Return from Tomorrow*. Lincoln, VA: Chosen Books, 1978.

Sabom, Michael B. *Recollection of Death*. New York: HarperCollins, 1982.

Sai Baba. *Sadhana, The Inward Path*. Brindavan, Bangalore: Sri Sathya Sai Education and Publication Foundation, nd.

Sallis, John, and Kenneth Maly. *Heraclitean Fragments*. University of Alabama Press, 1980.

Sandweiss, Samuel. *Sai Baba the Holy Man . . . And the Psychiatrist*. San Diego: Birth Day Publishing, 1975.

Schmaltz, Gustav. *Das Machen der Wahrheit im eigenen Herzen (Augustinus) und die dialektische Funktion des Unbewussten im Individuationsprozess [Meditation in Religion und Psychotherapie]*. Stuttgart, 1958.

———. *Oestliche Weisheit und Westliche Psychotherapie*. Stuttgart: Hippokrates Verlag, 1953.

Schultz, I. H., and W. Luthe. *Autogenic Training*. New York: Grune & Stratton, 1951.

Schwaller de Lubicz, Isha. *The Opening of the Way*. Rochester, VT: Inner Traditions, 1985.

Serrano, Miguel. *C. G. Jung and Herman Hesse: A Record of Two Friendships*. New York: Schocken Books, 1966.

Silva, Jose. *The Silva Mind Control Method*. New York: Pocket Books, 1977.

Spiegel, Herbert, M.D. and David Spiegel, M.D. *Clinical Uses of Hypnosis: Trance and Treatment*. New York: Basic Books, 1978.

Stearn, Jess. *A Matter of Immortality: Dramatic Evidence of Survival*. New York: Atheneum, 1976.

Stevenson, Ian. *Twenty Cases Suggestive of Reincarnation*. Charlottesville, VA: University Press of Virginia, 1980.

Talbot, Michael. *Mysticism and the New Physics*. New York: Bantam, 1981.

Toben, Bob. *Space, Time & Beyond*. New York: Bantam, 1983.

Weitzenhoffer, André M. *General Techniques of Hypnotism.* New York: Grune & Stratton, 1957.

von Weizsäker, Carl Friedrich. *Der Garten des Menschlichen.* München & Wien: Hanser Verlag, 1978.

Wilber, Ken. *The Atman Project.* Wheaton, IL: Quest Theosophical Publishing House, 1980.

Williams, J. Paul. "Belief in a Future Life," in *Yale Review.* Spring, 1945, p. 283.

Yogananda, Paramahansa. *Autobiography of a Yogi.* New York: Philosophical Library, 1951.

———. *Man's Eternal Quest.* Los Angeles: Self-Realization Fellowship, 1975.

INDEX

Eugene Jussek earned his medical degree at the Goethe University in Frankfurt am Main, and specialized at the University Hospitals in internal medicine and psychosomatics in the Jung tradition. After his board certification in internal medicine, Jussek supplemented his training with postgraduate work at different hospitals in the U.S.A., including the Bellevue Medical Center in New York. He considers mind, body, and soul as a whole, and frequently uses hypnosis as an adjunctive form of therapy as well as for behavior modification. Dr. Jussek has been internationally acclaimed for his pioneering work in biological healing methods. He lives and works in California.